The Essential Knuth

Donald E. Knuth
Edgar G. Daylight

Conducted by Edgar G. Daylight
on November 23, 2012, in Frankfurt, Germany.
Edited by Kurt De Grave.

LONELY SCHOLAR™
SCIENTIFIC BOOKS

First edition
Version 1.0.1

© 2013 Edgar G. Daylight
Cover design © 2013 Kurt De Grave
Cover photo © 2012 Rajan P. Parrikar
Photo Fig. 5.1 © 1975 Jill Knuth

Daylight can be contacted at egdaylight@dijkstrascry.com.

Published by Lonely Scholar bvba
Sint-Lambertusstraat 3
3001 Heverlee
Belgium
http://www.lonelyscholar.com

Typeset in LaTeX

D/2013/12.695/1
ISBN 978-94-9138-603-9
ISSN 2034-5976
NUR 980, 686

Contents

Preface

Approaching him seemed impossible. I had to wait my turn. Swarmed by admirers, Donald E. Knuth was struggling not to spill his drink at a reception in honor of Alan M. Turing. The rain outside and the fact that it was a summer day (June 22, 2012) meant that we were somewhere in England.

I walked around a bit, took another glass of champagne, and bumped into Bertrand Meyer. We talked about Agile Methods and Edsger W. Dijkstra. Bertrand had a big camera around his neck and at some point he asked me to hold his glass (which I did) so that he could take some fifty snapshots a second of a tall man standing on the window sill. It was Donald Knuth who had moved from one side of the chamber to the other in order to view the Olympic torch that was passing through Manchester. Bertrand was, just like me, waiting to approach Knuth at the right moment.

Realizing that my turn would not come automatically, I stepped forward and introduced myself to Knuth. He knew who I was by name and that I wanted his feedback on my research — I had taken care of that by sending him my book *The Dawn of Software Engineering: from Turing to Dijkstra* [17]. After listening to him for about an hour, I realized that an in-depth interview would serve my cause for the history of computing even better.

A few weeks later I sent my booklet on Peter Naur [16] to Don Knuth and requested an interview with him. He accepted and we met at Schloss Dagstuhl in Wadern, Germany on November 22, 2012. I drove Don and his lovely wife Jill to a hotel in Frankfurt where he and I got down to discussing the past. The interview led to the transcript presented in the sequel.

The transcript is mostly ordered chronologically. It starts briefly with Knuth's childhood and some of his avocations, music and physics. The first topic of major concern is his early encounters with computer programming. How, when, and why did Alan Perlis's Internal Translator and Stan Poley's SOAP II assembly program influence Knuth's own programming work? How did Knuth view the programming language ALGOL 60? Which new style of programming did Knuth acquire after studying the BALGOL compiler?

Knuth was essentially living two separate lives. During daylight he ran down the visible and respectable lane of mathematics — a lane on which many a traveler equated elegance with a short proof. During nighttime, Knuth trod the unpaved road of computers and compilers. Passers-by were few in number and diverse in programming habits. Perlis and Poley, for example, had very different approaches to programming, as Knuth notes in the interview. It was the latter's elegant style that helped show Knuth the way ahead. Around 1960, Knuth began to associate the mathematical connotation of short and sweet with an elegant program.

On his honeymoon in 1961, Knuth discovered that the roads of mathematics and computer programs intersect. For, Jill was not only accompanied by her newly wed husband on their joint trip through Europe, but also by Noam Chomsky's book *Syntactic Structures* [7] which Knuth was studying eagerly. Chomsky showed Knuth how mathematics and computing can be practiced together. One year later, Knuth met Bob Floyd who would teach him that you really could use mathematical reasoning to understand computer programs. The early sixties thus not only brought Jill and Don Knuth officially together, it also married mathematics and programming.

A second topic — discussed throughout — is the relationship between Dijkstra, Naur, and Knuth; thereby following up on my conversation with Naur [16] in which the distinction between intuition and formal methods comes to the fore. What is Knuth's take on formalism? How does he compare Dijkstra's devotion to formal reasoning with Naur's plea for pluralism in software engineering?

Other recurring topics are: (i) the advent of logic, undecidability, and Turing machines in computing, (ii) the dichotomy between machine efficiency and generality (à la ALGOL 68), and (iii) the eternal quest for machine-independent programming (cf. Knuth's experiences with floating point arithmetic and TEX).

Structured Programming of course deserves separate attention. The 1972 book *Structured Programming* [14] — written by Dijkstra, Hoare, and Dahl — was, as Knuth explains, revolutionary in his thinking. In his 1974 article 'Structured Programming with go to Statements' [43], Knuth wanted to show that goto statements are sometimes consistent with well-understood structure and why in this context program manipulation systems sound promising. Many historical actors attached their own meaning to the words "structured programming", whence my interest in obtaining a brief comparison from Knuth between the views of Böhm, Brooks, Jacopini, and himself.

Knuth also mentions several software pioneers that he knew personally, ranging from the programmer Ned Irons to the logician Dana Scott. In the last part of the interview, Knuth compares the study of the history of computing with that of mathematics and science. A historian himself, he expresses his reservations about the trend of writing about history without any appeal to technical content.

My main purpose to embark on this project was to get Knuth's perspective on the past on paper, realizing full well that I would not be able to cover all of his technical contributions. There is thus plenty of room for further research. The history of computing is, in my opinion, badly in need of a critical mass. Moreover, historical accounts can drastically help computer professionals understand their own research problems. Therefore, I strongly encourage the reader to delve into the careers of Knuth and other software pioneers, and to share his or her findings with all of us. (And if you plan to do so, feel free to contact me so that we can study and document the past together!)

The dialogue presented in the sequel is by no means a one-day effort. It is based on my preparatory research in finding a suitable set of questions to ask and extensive revisions of the original transcript by Knuth, my colleague Kurt De Grave, and myself.

— Edgar G. Daylight
  June 2013, Leuven, Belgium

Biography

Donald Ervin Knuth was born on January 10, 1938, in Milwaukee, Wisconsin, USA. He received Bachelor's and Master's degrees in Mathematics from the Case Institute of Technology in 1960 and a Ph.D. degree in Mathematics from the California Institute of Technology in 1963. After working as an Assistant Professor of Mathematics and Associate Professor of Mathematics at the California Institute of Technology, he became Professor of Computer Science at Stanford University in 1968. Between 1960 and 1968, he also served as a consultant to the Burroughs Corporation in Pasadena, California. He has remained on the faculty of Stanford University up till this day, and is currently Professor of The Art of Computer Programming, Emeritus. Knuth has received several awards throughout his career, including the ACM Turing Award in 1974, the Kyoto Prize in 1996, and the BBVA Frontiers of Knowledge Award for Information and Computation Technologies in 2010.

1. Childhood

Daylight: Your father was a school teacher and a good musician. In your recollections you state that your father saw you having some strange talents and that maybe he felt that he hadn't been successful enough himself [49, p.79].

Knuth: He was the first of his generation to go to college. He was always busy and doing things, always wanting to improve. His mood was generally upbeat, but I suppose underneath the surface there was also some anxiety. The things that he would worry about were mostly related to his work for Church-supported institutions, when he was keeping their books; he knew that his employers didn't have enough money, so he would often decide to reduce his own salary without telling anyone about it. He would worry about not making ends meet, much more than about not having had a more thorough education. He did in fact take some advanced courses in accounting, to improve on what he knew.

The main difference between his life and my own was that he was always involved to the hilt with local things, doing things for the people that he knew. I had more of a calling to global things; I'm mostly thinking about what I can do for people who live far away, people that I'll never meet. So I don't have much time to be a volunteer like my father. In a way I've been selfish, because the things that I do tend to be recognized widely, while he worked tirelessly in a small community. He was the kind of a person who provides the "lubrication" that's necessary to make the world work. Furthermore, the things I do don't scale up; there isn't a need for ten of me in the world.

You asked only about my father, but my mother was equally a vital force in my home town. She was prominent in real estate, especially with respect to managing some of the largest commercial buildings in downtown Milwaukee, and she also was an active volunteer for many local groups. She continued to work professionally until her death at age 89; my father passed away at a comparatively young age (62).

Daylight: Did your parents support you, encourage you?

Knuth: Absolutely. They read all the books on how to be good parents. They made sure that I could go to camp and art school in addition to my normal schooling. I even went to summer schools in order to learn shorthand and high-speed typing.

My parents were careful not to promote me a grade ahead. They believed, and rightly, that it was better for me to stay with people my own age and to do extra work outside of school.

Daylight: You also wrote that, as a school boy, you felt you had to prove yourself.

Knuth: Right.

Daylight: Is it then correct to describe you as a perfectionist?

Knuth: Well, I certainly can't argue with you about that! I don't know how early on I had this tendency, because I didn't know what perfection meant when I was younger. But I always thought that I could do better.

Daylight: There are many anecdotes about you. Perhaps we can discuss two of them: the anecdote about the library, and another about you as scorekeeper for basketball games.

Knuth: There was a bookworm club run by the Milwaukee library. Our newspaper once printed a paragraph about how I happened to be the youngest member of that club, at the age of two. So it's clear that I was already very interested in reading books almost from the start.

I grew up in halcyon days before there were problems with drug culture and vandalism, so young children could ride the public trams and go downtown by themselves. According to my parents, I therefore once took the tram to the library, when I was five years old or so, in order to follow one of the book reading sessions. I went to the place where I knew the books were, and I started to read. Then the lights went off; so I went over to the window in order to continue. I didn't realize that it was past closing time. Meanwhile my parents were wondering why I hadn't come home. They called the library, and somebody answered the phone and found me reading by the window.

Today it occurs to me that this episode was something like the story of Jesus in the temple, where his parents were looking for him on the way back from Jerusalem and he wasn't there with the crowd. Mary and Joseph had to return to the city, where they found him talking with the rabbis [K&D: Laughter] . . .

I was certainly fascinated by books, and my parents encouraged that interest. Yet they were actually somewhat worried, because the standard advice at that time was that a child who learns to read before going to school will be bored when classes begin, thus ruined for life. So they took flack from their friends for allowing me to read.

I also remember learning to read sort of on my own. My parents didn't have enough money to buy a car, but I once was riding with one of my uncles in his car, and we happened to pass an advertisement for Coca Cola. I remember observing that "this sign for Coca Cola is nicer than the usual ones, because it says 'Please drink Coca Cola'". Well, the sign actually said "Pause; drink Coca Cola," which was the slogan of the year for Coca Cola at that time. I didn't know enough to read it properly; and as a good little boy I had been taught to say "Please". That's my earliest recollection of reading. [K&D: Laughter]

Daylight: Jumping all the way to your late teens, you became the scorekeeper for the basketball team of your college.

Knuth: I started as a manager of the freshman basketball team in late 1956, and in fact I had worked with basketball teams in high school for three or four years. I was manager also of the baseball team and the football team. Thus I was a "letterman" in sports without really doing much athletics.

Daylight: Did managing entail more than score keeping?

Knuth: It was mostly score keeping in those days, but you also had to keep track of the uniforms and things like that when going on a trip. In basketball my main job was to sit at the scoring table and record how many fouls everybody had committed and how many points they had made. In baseball I had to record whether there was a hit to left or right field, how many strikes and balls were called, and so on. All these statistics had to be accumulated and totalled. I guess that was my introduction to applied mathematics.

The most interesting part of my college experience with basketball came during my junior and senior years, when I used computers to process the statistics in new ways. That application of technology to basketball led to a short film "The Electronic Coach," which was shown on national television and is now viewable on YouTube. (See [50, Chapter 23].)

Daylight: Sports is important in American education. Did you do any sports yourself?

Knuth: I was on a basketball team when I was in seventh and eighth grade, but I was part of the third string. My left hand didn't know what my right hand was doing. I couldn't get rebounds, I couldn't make the shots, and so on. I was tall but I wasn't very ... If we were real far behind, they would let me play, because it wouldn't matter. [K&D: Laughter] So that was embarrassing, but it didn't bother me too much. I was never very aware of social norms. For some kids the social pressure is very strong, but that never was too important to me. I just liked to have fun with my friends and wasn't worried about prestige.

I enjoyed working by myself on mathematics, but my teachers did not know much about the subject. I especially enjoyed drawing graphs. My dad had a mechanical calculating machine, so I used to help make more than a hundred graphs. For instance, I would write down $f = a + bx + cx^2 + dx^3$ and then I would vary a, b, c, and d, and I'd draw the resulting curves with different colors of pencil. In this way I learned how the shapes corresponded to the numbers. The graph paper was a small grid with orange-colored squares, and I think I started to get headaches because it wasn't good for my eyes.

We also had a little racetrack game, which featured six horses going around in a circle. I would roll dice and move one horse, then roll again and move another horse, and so on. I would root for the red horse to beat the blue horse. So I was empirically learning about statistics, getting a feel for the ways in which random numbers behave. I kept those horses under my bed for quite a while and played with them frequently.

Among other funny hobbies, I also went part-time to art school. I wasn't a good artist, but I thought it would be interesting to use oil paints and to make sculptures and so on. I was very bad at it, but I just enjoyed trying such things all the time. My parents supported all these activities.

2. College

Daylight: Going to college meant choosing between music and physics.

Knuth: Yes, music was another special avocation. I began piano lessons at age seven and continued through high school, when I also played saxophone and/or tuba in the band. I even arranged some music for my high school band to play. The director never used any of it, however, so that was a disappointment.

At the time I didn't know anything about plagiarism, so I was borrowing freely from all kinds of stuff that I found in books. For example, I spent several months writing a take-off on Prokofiev's *Peter and the Wolf*. I was a fan of the humorist Roger Price, who had written a book called *In One Head and Out the Other*, containing a story about *Milton and the Rhinoceros*. So I set the words of Price's *Milton and the Rhinoceros* to the music of Prokofiev's *Peter and the Wolf* and arranged it for our band. It was supposed to be hilarious, at least with respect to my sophomoric sense of humor. I orchestrated it quite carefully and I copied all the parts out laboriously and gave the manuscript to my band director very proudly. But alas, I never saw it again. He said he was going to show it to a publisher but, anyway, it has disappeared. That was my experience with music in high school.

On the other hand, I had a great chemistry and physics teacher. (The math teacher was not very good.) I went to Case as a physics major because I was inspired by this teacher and also because I thought physics was going to be an interesting challenge.

Daylight: These are very diverse interests. So how did your sister view your activities?

Knuth: She is more than three years younger than I am. She was always expected to excel as I had been doing, so she felt bad about that. But she came first in her class when she was a senior. We always have been good friends. Three years is actually a big difference when you are young.

Daylight: Did your parents set you as an example for your sister?

Knuth: Yes. I was certainly off the charts. My school didn't give letter grades but they gave percentages. My overall percentage in high school was 97.5% or so, which I think was an all-time record. I didn't realize it but I had sort of been taught how to be a good boy. I was supposed to get 100% on the exams, and if I didn't get everything right I'd have to study harder. [D: Laughter] I was pretty much a machine, doing what I was told.

Daylight: At some age you must have started to realize that you were really very good.

Knuth: I had passed the exam to get into Case Institute, which was very selective. It was not as selective as Caltech but it was one of the most selective in the country. So they admitted me to the honors section, a special section that was going to be taught by their best professors. I must have looked good to them at the time. But the funny thing was that the vice-principal of my school spoke to me before I graduated and said "Well Don, you've been successful at high school but you're going to be a failure in college. You just can't keep this up." I don't know why he told me this. Then I get to college, and the week before classes started the dean said, "OK everybody, listen up. This is a tough school. Look to the guy on your left, look to the guy on your right. One of you isn't going to be here next year."

I was scared stiff. I spent all my time studying. If the math teacher assigned five problems out of twenty, then I would do all twenty. I stopped playing ping pong and bridge because I wasn't doing quite well enough in my classes.

That approach turned out to be quite a wonderful strategy because, after I'd done twenty problems, I understood how to do problems; thus I could cruise through the later parts of the course, and everything became easy. I had started by working hard and learning the way to do it, so later I had extra time to do other things as well, joining student organizations.

Daylight: How did you learn? Did you mainly do exercises or did you sometimes literally copy a whole chapter on paper?

Knuth: I guess it was mostly by reading and doing the supplementary exercises in the book. I had good teachers and I just followed what they told me to do. But later on I started reading history, for example, when I got into mathematics. I had learned Latin in high school, so I started to read Fermat's writings in Latin.

Daylight: When was this?

Knuth: I was a sophomore or junior in college. I remember how interesting it was to see how Fermat would express formulas in words instead of in symbols. He would say "adaequabatur", which meant "approximately equal to", and things like that. I could psych out his meaning by seeing his words. I got fascinated by such things and did them on my own, outside of class.

Daylight: Was there a setback that you recall? So far it seems like all went well.

Knuth: What didn't go well was welding — and other work with my hands, as in chemistry lab. I also ran for student government and that didn't work.

I kept trying stuff. I would often be writing things that were supposed to be humorous. I was active in Theta Chi fraternity, where I had my closest friends. And of course I was learning a little bit about girls. I was very naïve and it took me many years before I kissed a girl.

Daylight: Because you were doing well in school and later in college, you must have started to feel very confident.

Knuth: I started to feel confident in a way, but I failed to impress Professor Guenther. He was my maths teacher. I would work very hard and I would show him something and he would just say "Oh." I worked really hard for him, doing all the supplementary exercises and things like that.

Daylight: Did you meet him afterward?

Knuth: By the time I was a senior he grudgingly admitted that I was okay.

Daylight: Can you say something about Louie Green and your early encounters with computer programming?

Knuth: Professor Green was famous because he had once flunked an entire class. He's the one who taught his own course on discrete mathematics, making up the syllabus himself. It turned out that discrete mathematics was what I was really born to do, that and computing. I began to major in mathematics instead of physics, largely because of his class. But he hated computers.

I fell in love with the IBM machine that Case had recently acquired. It arrived early in my freshman year, at the beginning of 1957. I saw it through a window and somebody told me how to use it. I learned first how to write a program, not in machine language but in what was called the Bell Interpretive System. Later I learned that this system had been modeled on Backus's Speedcoding.

The Bell System simulated a computer in which ten decimal digits constituted an instruction. For example, one digit was the operation code; and if it was the code for addition the instruction would compute the sum of two numbers, using three digits for the address for A, another three digits for B, and the last three digits for C. The machine would then add the contents of A and B and store the result in C. I wrote my first program in that language, which was numerical (not algebraic) and interpreted, as if we had a virtual machine.

I was actually a fraternity pledge at that time, and I wrote the program on behalf of one of the brothers who needed to solve some fifth-degree equations. From my previous experience drawing graphs, I knew that a polynomial of odd degree has to cross zero somewhere. Thus I could find one root by some kind of a binary search. After one root was known, the other four could be found by solving a fourth-degree equation, for which I found formulas in a book. I programmed all of that in the Bell language and, as far as I know, it worked.

Figure 2.1: Young Donald Knuth, age 20, at his first IBM 650 computer in 1958. Photo by Case News Service.

I learned machine language in the spring from George Haynam, who was a staff member at the computer center. He would befriend people like me and show us what goes on inside the machine. Immediately I was hooked: I found that computers made sense to me.

The IBM user manual included several examples that seemed to be obviously awkward and bad. Here I was, a freshman, yet I could apparently use the machine much better than the author of that manual had recommended. This experience gave me confidence that I could write computer programs — not realizing at the time that almost any competent person could have improved upon those clumsy examples.

I had to support myself because my scholarship covered only part of my tuition. I had a job at the computing center, running the sorter. I was supposed to sort cards and tabulate statistics for one of the professors. And that gave me access to the computer on the other floor. Then, after I learned machine language, they let me work at the 650 console during the night. I think it was probably in the spring of that year that I wrote my first programs in machine language. I would stay up all night, debugging them. Bugs were numerous.

That was 1957. Other people whom you have interviewed, like Dijkstra and Naur and so on, were already several years ahead in experience by that time.

Daylight: Louie Green gave an unsolvable problem to you and your fellow students.

Knuth: Well, we thought his problem was unsolvable, because he offered an automatic 'A' grade to anybody who could solve it. Maybe he himself thought the problem was too hard to solve; we'll never know.

Daylight: That problem led you eventually to programming.

Knuth: No, it was independent of that. His problem came in the fall, while I had already been programming extensively during the summer. I wrote machine language programs for prime factorization, base conversion, and tic-tac-toe much earlier; tic-tac-toe was in June 1957. I wasn't taking Louie Green's class until September. And I figured out how to resolve his problem in November, without using a computer in any way.

Daylight: Were you trying to understand what this machine could do for you in different contexts? The three programs you just mentioned seem very diverse, are they not?

Knuth: Well, the first two programs had to do with things that I knew about math. The third one was playing a game. So here I was trying to think about learning, because I had built in a learning system.

I first needed to understand how many different positions can occur in a tic-tac-toe game. You can have up to five X's and four

O's, and then there are blanks. The memory of this machine consisted of only 2000 ten-digit numbers. Thus, the total number of positions in tic-tac-toe was about one-third of the total number of digits in the entire memory, leaving almost no room for my program. So I had to throw out symmetries to save a factor of about eight, in order to represent each position with one digit in the memory. I had to figure out how to take a position of X's and O's and normalize it so that, for example, a position and its 90-degree rotation would be recognized as the same thing.

Then I needed a method that would incorporate some elementary learning. I had one digit in memory for every inequivalent position. This digit would start out at 4, say; and if it corresponded to a position that I won, I would increase it (unless it was already 9), but if I lost I would decrease it (unless it was already 0). At the end of the game, all the positions for the winner would go up and all the positions for the loser would go down. And if it was a tie game, they would all move towards 4. It took a month to write that program and get it working.

Daylight: So you first looked at all combinations and then you realized that the memory was too small.

Knuth: Part of the task was to pack a table of all possible positions into the IBM 650's memory, which was small. But we didn't know at the time that our machine was small, because it was all we had. I was intrigued by that challenge.

I wrote three versions of tic-tac-toe. First I just built in a canned strategy, saying "OK, if you've got the first move, then move in the center. And if the opponent responds in the corner, then you move in the opposite corner." I had a complete strategy built into that version of the program, which I called Brain I. Then I wrote Brain II, which looked over all its possible moves at each step and tried to pick the best one, using just the rules of the game instead of expert advice. I got those versions to work, but then I thought "well, what about learning?" That led me to write Brain III. The trickiest part was to get Brain III to play against Brain I or Brain II instead of against a human opponent, or even to have Brain III play against itself, with "the blind leading the blind."

By the way, the reason I chose tic-tac-toe was because I had seen an exhibit put on by AT&T, in Chicago's Museum of Science and Technology. They had devised a tic-tac-toe demonstration where you could play against their machine. My previous encounter with that device in Chicago gave me the idea to write a program for Case students to play against.[1]

Daylight: This was still in 1957. Did you read what others were doing at that time?

Knuth: No, there was no general awareness of programming in our part of the world until the ACM began to publish the *Communications* in 1958; and I didn't see that monthly magazine until 1959, when copies appeared on people's desks in the computer lab. In 1957 I had seen just the user manual for our machine. I didn't know what was going on at MIT or elsewhere. I hadn't heard of Babbage or any other pioneers; I was completely unaware of all that.

But when we got the Internal Translator (IT) compiler from Carnegie Institute of Technology in the summer of 1957, it was a program that I couldn't imagine writing by myself. The miraculous behavior of IT seemed incredible to me. For example, I could punch a card that said 'X1 Z X2 S X3', where 'Z' meant equals and 'S' meant plus. (In those days input and output were done via punched cards, and only letters and digits could be represented on those cards; we had to encode the equation '$x_1 = x_2 + x_3$' as a sequence of letters and digits.) I would put that card in the machine and it would spin its lights and punch four other cards; and those cards would be *machine language*, to add x_2 to x_3 and store the result in x_1. I thought, "Wow, how did they do that?" A user could also write much more complicated algebraic expressions, using the letters 'L' and 'R' to stand for parentheses. A program that could understand parenthesized expressions went into uncharted territory, way beyond tic-tac-toe or anything else that I knew: The whole idea of parsing, of recognizing structure,

---

[1] I recently learned more about the Chicago exhibit, which had toured other museums and was based on early work by Bill Keister. His tic-tac-toe machine was not governed by a computer program, it was based in special-purpose hardware circuits built from relay switches, and he had designed it about 1940.

was completely different from finding prime numbers or playing a game.

I had to know how that was possible. So I got ahold of the source code for IT.

Daylight: Your learning system for tic-tac-toe seems rather advanced to me too.

Knuth: I didn't have any theory to rely on. The trick of having a digit to represent the desirability of each position just seemed to me that it might work. Of course other people had been experimenting with feedback ideas when training dogs, and so on. As a college freshman, I didn't know about such things; the approach that I took seemed like a fairly obvious way to proceed. In fact my program wasn't really that good at learning, but it was good enough to play a decent game.

Afterwards I learned that D. W. Davies had already written a program to learn tic-tac-toe in 1956, at England's National Physical Laboratory. He had described his method in a discussion on "The computer in a non-arithmetic role" during April of that year [9, p.473]. The learning mechanism of his program was better than mine, because it didn't prefer to make "safe" moves.

Daylight: When you came across the IT compiler, did you ask yourself whether there was anything the machine couldn't do?

Knuth: No. I wasn't that profound. I've never been very good at speculating about such things.

Daylight: The IT compiler was written by a team headed by Alan Perlis. Is it true that you only met Perlis in later years?

Knuth: I actually met him the following year, in 1958. Perlis's team at Carnegie invited a couple of us to go visit them. By that time a few of us students had made our own version of IT, which did tricks that weren't in Perlis's version, and we wanted to show it off.

Daylight: The IT compiler evidently made quite an impression on you. A similar remark holds for the later SOAP II, written by Stan Poley.

Knuth: Yes. I learned about SOAP II, Poley's assembly program, a month or two after I had seen IT. SOAP II has to be the most beautiful program ever written for the IBM 650. To read it was like watching a grandmaster play chess against a duffer. The instructions in this code came together beautifully. If the program had to do a job that could be done with only three instructions, then Poley had written those three instructions.

On the other hand the IT compiler might have used seven or eight instructions to achieve the same effect; the coding of that program always seemed awkward, probably because it was mindlessly produced from a flowchart. I figured out how IT recognized parentheses and how it kept track of structure in formulas, but the way in which it was programmed was ugly. Once I'd understood their algorithm, I asked myself why they hadn't also made better use of the machine.

Moreover, IT's team hadn't discovered an elegant way to do parsing. Their solution was based on looking at pairs of adjacent symbols and doing a kind of a table lookup with lots of goto's and everything. The approach seemed to work, but it was ad hoc, without any comprehensible pattern; Dijkstra would have called it spaghetti code. Perlis and his crew didn't know about the cellar principle that Bauer and Samelson had come up with, and which other people had invented in other ways. Their algorithm was inferior compared to the stacks that Turing and Dijkstra had.

After I learned how IT worked, and once I saw what beautiful code looked like, I naturally had to rewrite IT in a beautiful style, working with other students at the comp center. The result was a compiler that we called RUNCIBLE.

Daylight: You still used the same algorithm.

Knuth: Yes, we didn't know the algorithms of Bauer, Samelson, and others. The stack was very hidden in IT and RUNCIBLE. The bizarre method that we used, taken from IT but "on steroids," can be seen in a short paper I wrote at the time [34].

Daylight: Given that you and Perlis used the same algorithm, why was his style of programming less beautiful than yours?

Knuth: The IBM 650 had a two-word accumulator and its operation codes could do more than one thing at a time. For example, one operation code was called 'reset and add to the lower accumulator'. When you reset the accumulator, its upper half would become zero. Stan Poley's program would use the fact that the upper accumulator was resetting to zero while the lower accumulator was doing something else. Both aspects of the operation were useful simultaneously; the lower accumulator would get a value from memory and the resetting of the upper accumulator meant something too. Poley was a master at killing two birds with one stone. That's what I mean by using the machine well.

The machine had other instructions like 'store the data address', which meant that instead of storing the whole accumulator you'd just store part of it. In order to do that, you had to specify what was going to go into the other parts that weren't the data address; they had to be in the so-called distributor register. So Poley would just happen to have the right thing in the distributor and the right thing in the data address. Perlis would achieve the result by writing several instructions, some of them designed to compute the data address and others to get the right thing into the distributor. With Poley, everything was just in place. He made data flow seamlessly, and the computer could cruise right along.

Of course this is not the kind of elegance that we admire in higher level programming languages today.

Daylight: "Optimum coding" — was that terminology used?

Knuth: People did speak of optimum coding for the IBM 650, but in a different context: We used it to describe the best way to place instructions on the rotating drum, in order to avoid latency delays; only one of every fifty drum positions could be accessed at any particular time.

I guess we call Poley's style "optimized coding" now. Yet a compiler with -O20 optimization might not actually do as well. Poley obviously had considered many possible ways to write his code in machine language. Similar opportunities present themselves also in a high level language, because you can generally express an algorithm in many different ways, some of which are going to be harder for the compiler to match to the machine's capabilities. A simple example: You can often branch either on $x \neq y$ or $x > y$. In certain contexts, it's easier to test 'unequal to y' than to test 'greater than y', because in the latter case you may have to subtract y from x and check for overflow. Hence, $x \neq y$ might lead to faster machine code. The compiler doesn't know all the options that the programmer has available, because there always are many ways to write a program. Poley must have thought about the possibilities and selected one that actually was also friendly to the neighboring instructions.

Daylight: It's how all the instructions fit together, how they create a harmony.

Knuth: Yes, that style meant something to me. Poley's style was smooth, Perlis's style was clunky.

Daylight: Have you come across the programming styles of Willem van der Poel and Alan Turing? How would you describe their styles?

Knuth: I met van der Poel much later, but only for a short conversation. I've never studied his programs. Concerning Turing, I haven't looked at his machine-language programs.

I did read Turing's 1936 paper 'On Computable Numbers' [63] fairly early on. One of my undergraduate classes used Martin Davis's book *Computability and Unsolvability* [15], in which that paper is mentioned. My files at home contain a xerox copy of the paper, and xerox machines were rare or nonexistent when I was an undergraduate. So I probably read it at Caltech in the early 1960s.

I annotated my copy of Turing's paper with all of the errors that I found, together with ways to correct them. (Interestingly, a few errors had also been noted by someone else, who had written corrections into the library copy from which my xeroxed version was made.) As I'm reading your book on Peter Naur [16], I guess maybe I should go back and check if I caught the same errors that Peter has found.

I don't recall being struck either positively or negatively by Turing's programming style in that paper. He used what we now call macros, named with letters in Fraktur type(!) and accompanied by informal descriptions, and those conventions were admirably suited to his purposes. He sometimes was inconsistent when using the word 'None'. Of course errors are to be expected in a pioneering work of this kind, with no physical machine on which to check the programs that he wrote.

Daylight: After the RUNCIBLE compiler, you worked on the SuperSoap assembler in 1959.

Knuth: SOAP was an acronym for "Symbolic Optimum Assembly Program". And there was a popular radio commercial about a special laundry detergent called Super Suds. That detergent inspired the name "SuperSoap" for a program that was better than all the other SOAPs in terms of features. The IBM 650 had started to become baroque and later versions of the hardware included a small core memory: Besides the 2000-word drum, we now had 60 words of random access memory, worth the price of gold because they provided 600 more digits of memory without latency delays. The designers also added index registers and floating point arithmetic. For all these things, we needed an assembler that was smarter. I also added facilities to allow hand-specification of drum levels to decrease latency times. Thus SuperSoap had a whole bunch of new features that had never before been incorporated into an assembly program.

3. ALGOL

Daylight: In 1960 you graduated from Case Institute in Cleveland and moved to Caltech in Pasadena to major in Mathematics. To earn money, you first negotiated and then worked for Burroughs as a consultant, implementing ALGOL on the Burroughs 205. Then when you started to implement ALGOL, you apparently bumped into "a real problem", the runtime library [49, p.121].

Knuth: Yes, Burroughs didn't have a runtime library for the 205, and I'd had no idea that such a library would be part of my responsibility. I had to spend an extra month writing subroutines for sine, cosine, logarithms, and so forth.

The IT compiler had come to us with a runtime library — a set of punched cards to be loaded together with each user's program. And the analogous library for our improved system RUNCIBLE was written by other people at Case, mostly using routines developed at Bell Labs. When I made a proposal to Burroughs to write an ALGOL compiler, I naturally expected that Burroughs would already have a similar library already in place. But apparently nobody had yet written floating-point routines to compute standard mathematical functions on the 205.

Daylight: Had you come across FORTRAN by that time?

Knuth: In 1959 there was a ForTransit program, which took FORTRAN source and converted it to IT. Nobody at Case used ForTransit, because RUNCIBLE was much better.

Daylight: Why was programming the runtime library a difficult task?

Knuth: That task meant writing lots of code and debugging numerical subroutines, which is very difficult because you have many cases to consider. Numerous exceptions need to be handled within the code for exponentials, logarithms, square root; trigonometry also involves delicate reduction of ranges. I had to build all those routines, each of which should have been done by kind of a specialist. Since many different cases can arise, all kinds of subtle bugs are possible. When something goes wrong after you build a complex system, you usually don't know at what level the error occurred.

My task with the library wasn't hopeless, however, because I already had written much of the necessary code. Before I had the contract from Burroughs to write the ALGOL compiler, I had written a program for Cleveland Graphite Bronze Cooperation, a company that manufactured ball bearings. They were replacing their IBM 650 with a Burroughs 205. Their engineers wanted to convert a load study program, which was written in the Bell Interpretive System, into an equivalent routine for the 205. As part of this work I needed to write subroutines to handle the necessary floating-point functions.

Alas: I couldn't get the same answers as their program was producing! Since my floating-point subroutines had been written from scratch, I figured that I must have screwed up somewhere in that new code; but I was unable to find any bugs. Finally I broke down and traced both programs, theirs and mine, comparing the intermediate results at each and every step of the computation. And it turned out that their program contained an extremely serious bug, because of which they had never gotten correct answers at any time in the past! At one point in the middle of the computation, their program replaced a crucial number by a ten-digit instruction from the Bell Interpretive System, thus clobbering the data. It wasn't easy for me to convince them to trust the answers that were produced by my program on the 205, even though those answers differed substantially from the results they had obtained with the IBM 650.

Daylight: In his 1958 book, *Computability and Unsolvability,* Martin Davis tried to connect theory (Turing machines) to computing machines. You referred to his book in your 1961 article called 'Algol 60 Confidential'. You wrote:

> In fact, using GPS we can actually compute any computable function (see [Martin Davis's *Computability and Unsolvability*]), using a single ALGOL assignment statement. [47, p.112]

Knuth: This quote refers to an innocuous little subroutine that I'd called GPS for General Problem Solver, because the rules of ALGOL made that subroutine unexpectedly powerful.

As mentioned earlier, I'd had some exposure to computability theory through Davis's book, because of a course I'd taken during my senior year at Case. It was one of the optional courses and the subject matter was interesting, but computability theory didn't really rub off on me. For example, the book gave elaborate constructions of Gödel numbers; but nobody would ever use Gödel numbers in practice. Gödel numbers get way too big.

Even before 1960, as an undergraduate, I had however submitted a paper that proved something about some kind of abstract automaton. That paper was never published, and I think the referees had good reasons for rejecting it.

Daylight: In your work on ALGOL we again come across "elegance". You built an "Elegant Assembly SYstem" (EASY) and the "Most Elegant Assembly System Yet" (MEASY).

Knuth: In those cases elegance meant short. At this point in my mathematically oriented life, I was strongly influenced by Raymond Wilder's book *Introduction to the Foundations of Mathematics* [66], which taught me about axioms and showed how to prove things from undefined premises. Wilder introduced me to new worlds of complete abstraction where you can make up your own rules. The axioms are assumed to be true and if the axioms are true then such and such follows.

I spent a month at Case devising what I called the cosmoframmic system. First I defined the concept of a "cosmoframmic," probably using a word that I'd found in *MAD* Magazine or in one of its clones. Then I defined frammic operations, and eventually I proved a theorem that said "The absitive of the posilute of two cosmoframmics is equal to the posilute of their absitives" (see [1, p.188]). I proudly wrote these words on a big sheet of paper and posted it on the wall of my dormitory room. It was fascinating to be able to prove something rigorously about abstract concepts that were totally under my own control.

These experiences taught me the mathematical concept of elegance, meaning the construction of a short proof. I might discover a long proof or a short proof. Elegance meant short. So when I wrote my first assembly program for the Burroughs 205, I called it 'EASY' because the whole system consisted of less than 250 lines of code.[1]

Daylight: That's not so very different from the elegance that we have been discussing in connection with Stan Poley's work on SOAP II.

Knuth: Right.

Daylight: Was your study of axiom systems what we call universal algebra?

Knuth: Universal algebra is a special kind of axiom system, where the axioms are based on operators and substitution of variables. For a binary operator like $+$ you might introduce the axiom $a + b = b + a$. And then you can plug in any desired formula for a, and likewise for b. Universal algebra allows you to have any axioms you want that relate two such sequences of symbols. Besides binary operators you can also have unary operators (which apply to just a single variable), nullary operators (which are constants), ternary operators (which have three operands), and so on. But universal algebra doesn't allow axioms that correspond to the division operator in a field, where we might want to say that

---

[1] After the interview Knuth looked back at his files from those days and found the following note at the end of the one-page user manual for MEASY dated 24 August 1960: "P.S. There has been some question as the meaning of the word 'elegant' as used in EASY. This is to be taken in its mathematical connotation of 'short and sweet.' Excluding the OP-table entries the number of non-zero locations in the MEASY program is less than 300, including the format bands and the loading routine!" (MEASY extended EASY to produce output on magnetic tape and a line printer instead of punching cards.)

$(a/b) \times b = a$, because a/b is not allowed when $b = 0$. Universal algebra doesn't allow exceptions. All the rules have to apply always.

Daylight: Did you also check that your cosmoframmic axioms didn't contradict each other? Did you consider notions like consistency?

Knuth: Yes, and I also studied whether or not certain axioms were redundant, so that I might be able to deduce them from the others. I would thus try to find independent axioms. If you have four axioms, can you find a model that satisfies the first three but not the fourth one? If not, the fourth one is redundant, and you can do without it.

Four or five of us undergrads participated in an informal seminar at Case, for which Wilder's book [66] was sort of assigned reading. We read it and learned about axioms. Wilder was a prominent professor in Michigan.

Daylight: From Michigan, Ann Arbor?

Knuth: Yes. He wrote this paperback book that began with an excellent introduction to axiom systems. One of his main examples was related to finite projective planes, which later became the topic of my Ph.D. thesis.

Daylight: I wanted to ask you about John W. Carr, III, who was also at Ann Arbor.

Knuth: Carr was at Michigan in the early 1950s, and then he apparently went to North Carolina, according to your interview with Peter Naur. But I didn't know him at all until I met him in the late 1960s when he was at the University of Pennsylvania.

Then it was very unpleasant. I came through the door and he said "Why do you hate me?" or something like that.[2] He acted rather paranoid at that time, not friendly in any way. He didn't want to discuss any technical material. I think he wrote some really good things when he was at Michigan, in the summer schools during

_____

[2]Editor's note: Naur made a similar remark about Carr by referring to his 1961 encounter with him in North Carolina [16, p.22-23].

the 1950s. So the reception that I got from him shocked me when I finally met him in 1968 or 1969.

Daylight: I believe he was the president of the ACM in 1958.

Knuth: Thanks for the reminder. I don't know any more of his history, but I do know that my personal connection with him was very strange. The only explanation I can think of is that he probably had some kind of a breakdown. But I shouldn't really speculate, because I have almost no data.

Daylight: Burroughs wanted you to write four to eight versions of your ALGOL compiler, depending on different configurations of hardware [49, p.121].

Knuth: Yes; but that wasn't extremely difficult, because I only needed to substitute different I/O units or things like that. Burroughs had magnetic tape units on its high-end systems and paper tape units on its low-end systems, in addition to the ubiquitous punched cards. They also introduced a unique machine called the Datafile Multiple Bin Tape Unit, which contained fifty separate 250-foot lengths of magnetic tape within a single cabinet, allowing for more-or-less random access — somewhat akin to a disk drive, for which IBM had a monopoly. I mostly had to write new library subroutines and a few lines of code to handle input and output.

Daylight: In your flowcharts, did you localize those parts that changed from one hardware configuration to another?

Knuth: Not really; the flowcharts were for the compiler logic only. The only real problem that I had with multiple versions was that everything got really messy for customers who were forced to use paper tape. Paper tape was extremely unreliable: It would spill out all over the floor and then you would step on it and it would become unreadable. A huge long reel of paper tape was necessary to hold my compiler, and it would take a long time to read. Then the machine would come up with a parity error and you'd have to start all over again and rewind everything. Paper tape was a terrible nuisance, but the card systems were robust and fairly easy to change.

Daylight: Were you aware of what was going on in the UNCOL project?[3]

Knuth: We heard about it, but we didn't get enthusiastic because of the small computers we had. UNCOL was a forward looking thing that didn't "turn us on." I guess we were being too shortsighted. I never imagined computers getting bigger and faster. I always was optimizing for the machine that was in front of me, instead of foreseeing future trends.

Daylight: UNCOL researchers wanted to deal with the fact that machines were quickly becoming obsolete, and that hardware configurations were increasing in variety, and so on. This reminds me of the four to eight versions of your ALGOL compiler.

Knuth: Right, but that never dawned on me. I was just a boy doing his duty instead of leading a project.

Daylight: ALGOL was a machine-independent language for reasons similar to UNCOL's concept. Did ALGOL have a more profound influence on your thinking?

Knuth: ALGOL was nicer than any of the other languages that we had. I felt that it was a step forward, but I didn't imagine that more forward steps would occur later. I mean, I just thought, "OK, all computers are just going to be static". I don't know why I thought that. I just never bothered to ask such questions, which seem obvious today.

Daylight: Let's turn now to Robert Barton's BALGOL (with B for Burroughs). Your first task as a consultant for Burroughs in Pasadena was to write comments on the listing of the BALGOL compiler. In a sense, then, you had to reverse-engineer BALGOL.

Knuth: Most of BALGOL's authors were there at Burroughs in Pasadena, working for Barton, so I could ask them what they had done. I was extremely impressed with that compiler. I first saw it a couple months before I left Case.

---

[3]Editor's note: The Universal Computer-Oriented Language (UNCOL) was intended to enable working with any machine and for any computational purpose [59, p.62].

Daylight: We have discussed your encounters with Perlis's IT and Poley's SOAP II. Both systems made quite an impression on you. Was the same true for BALGOL?

Knuth: Absolutely. By that time I had written a couple of compilers myself, so I thought I knew all the tricks. When this strange new compiler (BALGOL) came to Case I said to myself "OK, let's see how bad it is." [D: Laughter] Giving it a short test program, using constants instead of variables because I wanted to look at the machine code, I asked it to calculate $25 - (5.0 \times 5.0)$ and store the result in Z.

Assuming that BALGOL was a run-of-the-mill compiler, I figured that it would start out by loading a register with the integer number 25; then it would call a library subroutine to convert that number to floating point. Then it would have to store the result temporarily, because the machine wasn't ready to do a subtraction until it had computed 5.0×5.0. The next step would typically be to compute that product; but the result wouldn't be usable immediately, because it appeared in a register, and the machine had no instruction to subtract a register from the contents of a memory location. (The subtraction operation went the other way, decreasing a register by the contents of memory.) Finally the subtraction would be achieved by loading 25.0 into a register and subtracting the floating-point product, and the result would go into memory location Z.

That's what I expected to see, or something worse. But when I looked at the machine language code generated by BALGOL, all it said was "clear location Z"! BALGOL was the first compiler that did constant propagation. It did everything at compile time. Not only that, it compiled about ten times faster [Knuth snaps his fingers] than any other compiler I had ever seen. I'd been saying to myself "This compilation is so darn fast, it can't possibly produce decent machine code." [He raises his voice in excitement.] But it produced better code than I'd ever seen before."

So you can see why I was so impressed by it. After I subsequently read the code and found out how such breakthroughs were possible, I had learned a brand new style of programming, involving linked lists of data. BALGOL's authors had used at least ten different kinds of lists. They had a stack to keep track of the parsing, and they had stacks for the variables that were involved, and for the storage allocation. They pushed things onto stacks and popped them off of stacks and did all sorts of insertion and deletion efficiently by using links instead of sequential memory. It was a revelation to me that you could process information with links so easily. Linked memory fit the machine architecture perfectly.

BALGOL was the first commercial software to use advanced data structures, after Newell, Shaw, and Simon had pioneered the ideas of list processing in their experimental programs for artificial intelligence. Joel Erdwinn was the main genius behind BALGOL. But I didn't get to meet him personally until several years later. By 1960 he had moved to Houston to work for Shell Oil; then he was hired by Computer Sciences Corporation, which was the first big software firm, a company in southern California. CSC started writing compilers for big bucks; for example, they wrote an innovative compiler for the UNIVAC LARC, a well-funded project at Livermore.

Daylight: The list processing was thus carried out at compile time. Does that mean that the compiler was written with what we today call dynamic memory management?

Knuth: Yes, things like that. They used modern data structures to do their processing. Before that, all compilers just had arrays, basically.

Daylight: Then came the Burroughs B5000 machine, where Barton and his team wanted to do as much as possible in hardware.

Knuth: Exactly. The company's philosophy was based on the idea that programmers were beginning to love high-level languages; thus it seemed wise to implement high-level operations directly in hardware. In other words, the Burroughs philosophy was precisely the opposite of RISC.[4] They wanted to do as much in hardware as they could, and they wanted their machine language

---

[4]RISC = Reduced Instruction Set Computing.

to be almost identical to ALGOL — except that the B5000 used Polish notation internally so that parentheses weren't needed.

Daylight: Were you skeptical about this?

Knuth: I had no opinion. I was a consultant and I did as I was told. I thought their approach was interesting, but at that time I wasn't the kind of guy who questioned the wisdom of stuff very much.

A few years later, however, some of the same people who had worked on BALGOL started doing some more far-out projects, whose methods were incomprehensible to me. Everybody seemed to be excited about those supposedly brilliant ideas, but I never understood why; the new project reminded me about the story of the emperor's new clothes. That project flopped, but I was never asked to participate in it. It was being done at another branch of Burroughs, far away in Paoli, Pennsylvania. I would occasionally hear people talking about the new ideas, but I never could fathom how those ideas would work. I was mildly concerned about that, but it wasn't my job to think about such things.

Edsger Dijkstra was a consultant for Burroughs in the 1960s. I met him several times when he came out to the Pasadena plant. I don't think he was involved in the failed Paoli project, though I don't know that for a fact.

Daylight: Can you tell a bit about Edsger's stay at your house in Stanford? Apparently there wasn't any electricity in your house.

Knuth: That's true, although I don't know how you learned about it!

Jill and I came to Stanford in 1969. Edsger stayed at our home, so we had obviously become good friends by that time. Besides his visits to Burroughs in Pasadena, we had met each other in Newcastle, spending a week in at least one of the legendary summer schools held there.

In September of 1969, Edsger visited Stanford and stayed with us. We had just moved into a rented house, after spending a year in Princeton, and we had yet to pay a deposit before the electricity could be turned on. Our things were still packed. Edsger slept on a makeshift bed.

We talked during the daytime, when there was light enough to see each other. He had recently learned about the System/360 machine language, and he told me seriously that his heart had started to flutter as he was reading the description of that IBM architecture.

Edsger's great strength was tied to the way he felt deeply about things. He was uncompromising, while I tend to be wishy-washy. He was profoundly sensitive, so much so that a bad design could even affect him physically. As a result he could do great things as he struggled hard to find truly good solutions to important problems.

Of course no one is always right, and so I didn't agree with him all the time. But I admired the clarity and the wisdom he had. Not only in computing. When you talked to Edsger about any subject whatsoever, he was like an encyclopedia. People remember him now for what he did and published about programming; but if you brought up any topic of conversation at dinner time, he would always know an awful lot about it that none of the rest of us did. He was very amazing. My main disagreement with him was that he decided not to use computers during the last 20 years of his life.

Daylight: Coming back to the B5000, Barton and other machine designers occupied part of the main floor in the Burroughs plant at Pasadena, whereas the machine builders were in the basement.

Knuth: Yes. The so-called product planning department was on the ground floor, and Barton was there during the first year of my stay. But then he moved to Paoli and started to lead that other project.

I was a consultant who could work on both floors. The people in the basement reported to a different person, who reported to a vice president who had comparatively little interaction with the vice president responsible for the planners on the main floor. In the company structure the closest intersection point between the basement and the main floor was actually somewhere in

Detroit! But I was a consultant to both groups, so I could pass information directly between the planners and the builders. I was also teaching classes to the hardware engineers (in the basement) about software.

Burroughs was in fact a very nice organization: Their engineers had a good spirit, and they had very good teamwork and managers. Unfortunately, however, the Burroughs salesmen were terrible. The salesmen didn't know the product, and they weren't knowledgeable about computers. They had mainly learned how to buy drinks for potential customers, so the situation was pathetic.

But my coworkers at Burroughs were very good colleagues indeed. I would spend half an hour with one guy and then half an hour with the next guy, roaming from one office to another and considering whether I knew anything that could help them with what they were doing. They would tell me what their problems were and I would pass that on to somebody else. My main function was communication.

I also debugged their designs. I took the designs home with me to see if I could find errors in them.

Daylight: When you say you took home the designs of the machine, are you referring to the logical specifications prepared by the hardware engineers in the basement who were building it?

Knuth: Yes. The product planners upstairs would say "We want to have a stack in the hardware," and "We also want the numbers to have a bit in them saying whether or not they are pointers or actual data," and similar things. These plans were radically different from any machine that had ever been built before. So the guys in the basement were interpreting these specifications without really knowing what they meant or what they were good for. When I looked through their designs, I naturally found cases where they hadn't understood the right thing to do.

In order to implement the stack, the engineers had to avoid wasting time unnecessarily by storing intermediate results in memory when they could keep it in a register. For instance, the ALGOL statement $x := y + z$ corresponds to pushing y and z onto the stack, adding them, and popping the result into x.

Ideally these operations would all be done in registers instead of actually "pushing" any data between storage locations in memory. Therefore the registers at the top of the stack were sometimes empty instead of having data. Complicated logic was needed to control what should happen when one register was empty and the other one wasn't. These newfangled ideas had to be implemented carefully; hence the hardware engineers needed direction. They needed help from somebody who knew about compilers.

Inside a computer there are a whole bunch of flip-flops, which contain the bits of data that are accessible at top speed. Some of those flip-flops form registers that hold numbers, and the adder is connected to those registers. Then there's less accessible memory, which is now called a cache, but at that time all numbers not in registers would have to be held in magnetic core storage. It takes time to store a number in core memory and to read it back. The stack might have 100 locations, of which only the first five might be in use at a particular time. The sixth location would then be reserved for the next item on the stack, but the computer would try to keep that item in a register if possible. In fact, the best scenario is to have the top two items in registers, when you want to add those two numbers together. But then after you've added them together, you have one result at the top of the stack, and the other register is empty. All of the different scenarios had to be handled properly, and all in hardware.

Daylight: Right, so the hardware engineers didn't really know what it was for.

Knuth: They had a glimmering, but they needed somebody to really check their work, because such things had never been done before. The other companies had a much more conventional idea of machine design. Conventional instructions were easy to synchronize, and you had only one way to perform them instead of multiple ways to achieve equivalent results. A hardware stack presents many choices as to what you should to do when pushing or popping the data. All of the different options would eventually produce the same answers at the end, but the engineers had to decide between various alternatives in each case. On a conventional machine an ADD instruction was much simpler;

it just would add the contents of one register to the contents of another, period.

Later, people found out that it was much better to avoid all these complexities in hardware, by letting compilers figure out what to do. A compiler can devise appropriate sequences of micro-instructions by looking at the context of each program statement. Complex software is easy, by comparison with the design of complex circuits that are able to handle all cases efficiently. A circuit can't look ahead and see what's coming next in the program, but a compiler can.

Daylight: In your article 'Algol 60 Confidential' you made several claims about how you perceived ALGOL at that time. For example, you wrote:

> ALGOL seems to have become too general. [47, p.103]
>
> There seems to be no need for such generality. [47, p.104]
>
> Of what value is this extra generality, when it actually causes machine implementations to be less efficient and the language to be more difficult to comprehend? [47, p.105]
>
> [B]ut extra things that are not needed have been put in. Those extras serve only to confuse [. . .] and they give more headaches to the people who are trying to write ALGOL translators. [47, p.113]

Knuth: Yes, efficiency was the gold standard for me.

Daylight: Van Wijngaarden was very much in favor of this generality.

Knuth: He loved it, yes. And ALGOL 68 took it to the hilt. It is very easy to become enamored of logical consequences without being enamored of efficiency. Once you get bitten by this bug, you can see all kinds of beautiful possibilities that are intellectually satisfying but economically tragic.

Of course not all abstract things are bad. It's fun to solve puzzles, so you look for new puzzles to solve. And when you've solved the puzzle, you feel satisfied. But not every puzzle deserves your attention. Puzzles are challenges, and so you rise to the challenge and feel satisfied, but random puzzles are rarely meaningful.

I recently read Peter Naur's critique of Dijkstra's "Pleasantness Problem" [16, p.77]. It's hard for any scientist to separate all the things that are going on in his or her mind at once. Dijkstra was trying to separate things into orthogonal parts, while Naur saw everything as a whole.

This is characteristic of computer science: I believe the thing that marks a computer scientist most is an ability to jump across levels of abstraction: We see the small and the large and several things in between as a continuum, and we don't even notice that we're jumping levels. But we know that, in order to accomplish some big goal, we have to modify some register at the lowest level. The people who are good at seeing the whole picture at once in this way tend to be really good programmers, but they tend not to be so good at separating things out into independent components.

I believe Dijkstra forced himself to decompose an idea into sub-ideas that were more or less independent; but Peter doesn't think that way. It seems to me that the clash between them was more in style of thinking than in what they really meant.

Like Edsger, Peter is a person whose strength lies in the strength of his opinions. As I said, I'm more wishy-washy. And I too am a good programmer; so I'm also unable to properly understand someone else's thought processes. There's no universal way to think about things, so I can't claim that someone else is thinking about something wrongly if they don't think about it the way I do.

Daylight: I believe you have referred to Dijkstra's THE multiprogramming system as a very elegant creation.

Knuth: He sent me the source code of THE, but I haven't read it yet. I'm much better at compilers than at operating systems.

Daylight: Dijkstra introduced separate levels of concern in his THE system. It's a precursor to his structured programming.

Knuth: Exactly. He was good at finding good abstractions. Peter [Naur] doesn't have that talent so strongly, it seems to me, but he admirably sees the whole picture in general.

While we're discussing Peter's views, I think you were right in your interview with him when you said you were going to be the Devil's advocate in connection with whether a synapse isn't really a memory [16, Chapter 17]. I agree that he somehow gets turned off by the word "memory", but he is talking about the equivalent of a memory. It's not exactly a computer memory but it's a neurological memory.

Daylight: Peter Naur was turned off by Dijkstra's 'Notes on Structured Programming' [19], some time around 1970.

Knuth: Yes, but Peter had his snapshots [56], which to me are similar to Floyd's paper on assertions [26].

Let me tell you my favorite Naur story. When I first met him, we had both been invited to Norway. It was 1967, right after the conference on simulation languages. We were invited to discuss the curriculum for teaching about computers in Norway. The discussion was to take place in Trondheim, but we wanted to visit the little village of Røros, which appears in stories by Johan Falkberget. Jill and I flew into Røros and met Peter there and got to know him. Then we had sessions in Trondheim where we were asked what should be in the Norwegian curriculum. This was before I had published my first volume of *The Art of Computer Programming* [39] and before Peter had invented the excellent name datalogy as an alternative to the term "computer science." We both presented our outlines regarding what we thought would be the best things for students to know. And our outlines were almost exactly identical! Both of us had come up with the same conception of how to teach computing.

My outline was divided into chapters that more-or-less constituted the table of contents for *The Art of Computer Programming*. Peter's was divided into chapters that became his notes on programming [57], which came out in the middle of the 1970s as he developed them. In 1967 our outlines were almost identical, and that impressed us a lot. That's how we became friends.

Daylight: I notice a lot of similarities between Naur and you, but I also notice that you frequently applied theory from Turing and Post in your research of the 1960s. That's something Naur didn't do at all. I don't think he would have wanted to include such theory in a curriculum on datalogy.

Knuth: I come from mathematics and he comes from astronomy. In mathematics people think about infinity. But my use of theory in the remark about GPS that you quoted earlier was just trying to show that nobody realized how powerful the call-by-name mechanism of ALGOL really was.

Daylight: You were giving the call-by-name mechanism a theoretical connotation.

Knuth: The examples that had previously been used for call-by-name were so tame that people didn't know what it was.

Amazingly, Dijkstra figured out how to implement it. The rest of us tore our hair out and had no idea how to do an implementation. The people implementing LISP didn't know how to handle the equivalent of call-by-name in their language. People called it the up-level addressing problem, and it was notorious for being impossible to implement. But Dijkstra invented his idea of the Display, which actually does the job, although it is tricky to get the details right. Nothing short of the Display will work.

Even today, hardly anybody realizes how hard it was to achieve this. I devised the GPS example as part of an attempt to illustrate some of the things that were hard to implement. By nesting one call of GPS in another, you could basically simulate a Turing machine; therefore you needed the Display.

Dijkstra's solution to the up-level addressing problem was not just recursion,[5] it was recursion together with changing the scope in the middle. He took parameters and encapsulated them so that they could retain their own scope in the midst of other scopes. In a sense, he carried recursion to an infinite power.

Thus the issue here is not a question of 'recursion' versus 'not recursion'. It's 'recursion with call-by-name' versus 'simple recursion'. Call-by-name made recursion not only difficult to implement, but also difficult to comprehend and to explain to a user.

───────────────

[5]Editor's note: It was not just recursion as Daylight suggests in Chapter 3 of [17].

Daylight: Did you get any reactions to this passage about GPS in your article 'Algol 60 Confidential'?

Knuth: Not that passage. I think Edsger did say about this article that it "wasn't written under the Christmas tree," or something similar. I don't know if that's a Dutch expression. He sort of said that, when Jack Merner and I wrote 'Algol 60 Confidential', we were not thinking friendly thoughts, we were sort of in-your-face. Our article had a belligerent tone that we didn't really intend.

Daylight: In your recollections, you've written about the two parallel paths that you were following. One path was your professional work — on combinatorial mathematics and formal theories — which occupied you during the day. The other path was your computer programming work, which you pursued mostly during the evenings. You've stressed that these "two worlds had essentially nothing in common" [49, p.123], and that they only started to converge during the 1960s. I guess this passage on GPS, in which you referred to Martin Davis's *Computability and Unsolvability*, was a first converging step.

Knuth: Yes, but it wasn't a significant step. I wouldn't call it a turning point in any sense. It was just an example of how baroque something can be, not a wake-up call that theory could actually improve my programming in practice. The turning point for me was reflected by my paper on what is now called the Knuth–Morris–Pratt algorithm [53], which was published in 1977 but actually based on earlier work done in 1971. It's about pattern matching in strings, where I found that automata theory could teach me how to do something that, as a programmer, I would never have thought of doing.

Daylight: In preparing this interview, I've missed your earlier work on automata theory, which is covered in your book the *Design of Algorithms* [48]. Therefore, the following is a preliminary list of articles in which you have referred to Post's correspondence problem [60], undecidable problems in general, Turing machines, the Halting Problem, and even to Cocke and Minsky's work on Tag Systems [8].

- 1965: 'On the Translation of Languages from Left to Right' [36]

- 1967: 'Top-down Syntax Analysis' [42]

- 1967: 'The Remaining Trouble Spots in ALGOL 60' [37]

- 1968: 'Semantics of Context-Free Languages' [38]

Knuth: These papers are not about automata theory. This is mathematics. When you talk about Martin Davis, you're talking about automata theory. The main conference about theoretical computer science used to be called 'Switching and Automata Theory' (SWAT). It's now called 'Foundations of Computer Science' (FOCS) or the 'Symposium on the Theory of Computing' (STOC), but originated as SWAT. My only personal connection to the things that Martin Davis and others were doing with computability was related to various kinds of parsing problems that are unsolvable. The ambiguity problem, for instance, is unsolvable.

But when we consider automata theory itself, as a key to doing things that I couldn't do with just my programming hat on, I first realized its value while working on pattern matching in strings. My paper on that topic [53] has now been reprinted, with additions and corrections, as Chapter 9 of the *Design of Algorithms* book [48]. Incidentally, I've dedicated that book to Bob Floyd.

Daylight: You have mentioned Chomsky as an important turning point [49, p.124].

Knuth: I heard about Chomsky from somebody when I was an undergraduate. So I got ahold of his book *Syntactic Structures* [7] and I took it with me on my honeymoon [in 1961]. Somebody at Case's computer lab told me about that book. Chomsky's theories fascinated me, because they were mathematical yet they could also be understood with my programmer's intuition. It was very curious because otherwise, as a mathematician, I was doing integrals or maybe was learning about Fermat's number theory, but I wasn't manipulating symbols the way I did when I was writing a compiler. With Chomsky, wow, I was actually doing mathematics and computer science simultaneously. But it was not Martin Davis's style of mathematics; to me it had a distinctly different feeling.

Daylight: You read Chomsky's book before you read the now-famous article 'On formal properties of simple phrase structure grammars' by Bar-Hillel, Perles, and Shamir [3]. Is that right?

Knuth: I didn't even know that such an article existed until much later.

Daylight: How did you bump into Post's work and his "correspondence problem" [60]?

Knuth: That must have been from the paper by Bar-Hillel et al. It was quite a revelation to me.

Daylight: Could you say something about Bob Floyd? I know very little about him.

Knuth: Well, he and Peter Naur had something very significant in common. They both were married to Christiane Floyd!

I first met Bob in Syracuse at the 1962 ACM convention. I had just finished writing a FORTRAN compiler for the UNIVAC solid state machines, and I had read a couple of papers that he had written. He was at this conference, representing Tom Cheatham's company Software Associates. We hit it off really well, and began to write letters back and forth. Shortly afterwards I went to visit him at his home in Massachusetts.

Floyd was self-taught. Before 1965 there had been essentially five really good papers written about compilers, in my opinion, and he had written four of them. (The other, I think, was by Ned Irons, although many other people had done significant work. Bob's masterful survey of the state of the art in 1964 [25] is part of my "top five" list.) He was a born computer scientist, and he also had unusually good insight into the structure of computation and parsing. He had invented precedence grammars and the idea of production systems for the recognition of context-free grammars [22]. We also discussed sorting algorithms and algorithms for the transitive closure of graphs — all different kinds of algorithms that we found fascinating. He and Tony Hoare had the Floyd–Hoare assertion method for proving programs correct.

Floyd was a child prodigy. His parents, unlike mine, did believe in pushing him ahead, so he found himself a graduate student at around age 14. He went to the University of Chicago as part of a program for exceptionally bright children. Then all of a sudden he crashed when he discovered he was a teenager and realized that there was a life to be lived. He never completed a degree. He took a job to program IBM 650 computers at Armour Research, which was kind of a think tank in Chicago. Being a natural computer scientist, he did well at that, and started to write important papers.

Daylight: When you met Floyd for the first time, did you have the impression that he was well aware of the work of Chomsky and Post?

Knuth: I don't recall.

Daylight: It's not that he gave you the references to Chomsky and Post?

Knuth: Not Chomsky; I don't remember how I learned about Post. Floyd did publish a result that ALGOL is not a context-free language [24]. What he really meant in that paper was this: If you add constraints to insist that every variable in an ALGOL program must be declared, then you can't express those constraints in a context-free grammar. Backus–Naur form (BNF) is a context-free grammar; but the question is, what is an ALGOL program? Is it something that satisfies the BNF in the ALGOL Report, or is it something that satisfies the BNF and also has the property that every variable is declared? With that extra condition, an ALGOL program is not expressible in BNF; so it's a side condition, and Floyd pointed that out. He probably used some existing theory to do that.

From whom did I learn about Post? I think it was Sheila Greibach or Seymour Ginsburg. They were the gurus for the theory of context-free languages. Sheila Greibach's Ph.D. thesis opened my eyes significantly when I read it.

Daylight: Floyd refers in his paper on ambiguity and unsolvability [23] to the paper of Bar-Hillel et al. [3].

Knuth: It's quite possible that I learned about that from Floyd. But it's also possible that I came across it independently, because I'd been thinking about ambiguity for so long.

I can definitely remember that Floyd and I discussed the ambiguity problem in 1962 in Syracuse. A special case of the ambiguity problem, when restricted to a finite-state language rather than in a context-free language, boils down to this: Suppose we have a bunch of different strings α_1, α_2, α_3, ... and then we write a sentence by concatenating copies of those particular strings. Afterwards we erase the boundaries between the copied strings. Which sets of strings have the property that it is always possible to figure out the boundaries again?

For instance if I start with simple strings that are all different, like *a*, *b*, and *cc*, then obviously when I write, say, *abcca*, then I know that it was made up of copies of the four strings *a*, *b*, *cc*, and *a*. I might also throw in another string like *ab*; but then it would not be clear whether *abcc* was made up of *a*, *b*, and *cc* or of *ab* and *cc*. Sardinas and Patterson [62] had worked out a simple way to decide whether or not ambiguities are possible in such a setting. Floyd had independently discovered the same algorithm, and we talked about it in 1962. I had played around with it too. I knew various conditions that were necessary and sufficient for being unambiguous. From Bar-Hillel et al.'s work, I could of course see that the ambiguity problem was unsolvable.

Daylight: In your recollections, you wrote about Chomsky and the ambiguity problem as follows:

> I presented context-free grammars and the ambiguity problem as the topic for my oral examination at Caltech. Math grad students were supposed to present some piece of original research, and the work that I presented was based on Chomsky's theory. Of course, I didn't solve the ambiguity problem that I'd started out to tackle. But I was able to solve some simple cases, and my partial results were of sufficient interest to become the subject of that oral exam. [49, p.156]

Knuth: That's right, at Caltech. We were supposed to do some independent studying. What I presented was my necessary and sufficient conditions, but I didn't show that the ambiguity problem was unsolvable.

Daylight: Did you know it was unsolvable? Did you think it was unsolvable?

Knuth: [Pause] I think I conjectured that it was solvable. I was hoping to solve it. And I had solved it in the case of a one-letter alphabet.

The important thing for me was that it was mathematics and it was computing at the same time. Floyd was the person who taught me that you really could use mathematical reasoning to understand computer programs. It might seem obvious now, but in fact almost everybody who wrote computer programs in those days had a mentality of "keep patching it until it seems to work". John Backus and other people of that vintage would say that their worst nightmare was that they would wake up in the morning and think of an example that their program didn't parse correctly, because they had no way of proving correctness. All they could do was think of reasons why it wasn't incorrect. Nobody else I knew thought that mathematical theory was relevant to programming practice. There might have been other people in the world who had such views, but not anybody whom I had met.

Daylight: Van Wijngaarden had a 1963 paper called 'Switching and Programming' [65], where he used axioms. Tony Hoare refers in his 1969 article 'An Axiomatic Basis for Computer Programming' [30] to van Wijngaarden's paper. Van Wijngaarden wasn't like Floyd trying to prove the correctness of programs, but he was connecting mathematics to programming. A similar remark holds for his 1962 paper 'Generalized ALGOL' [64].

Knuth: Semantics was the hot topic. One prominent approach, by de Bakker, defined semantics by adopting some things from van Wijngaarden, things that appeared later in ALGOL 68. It was the idea of generating new rules all the time, adding them to a dynamic list of rules. And every time, if you wanted to know what to do next, you looked at this list and took the topmost applicable rule. So when you put a new rule on the list, it could obsolete all the other ones.

I think such a method is horrible, because it doesn't map onto the human brain at all. A computer can follow such rules, but a human being cannot conceive of all the implications of a growing list of stuff, where suddenly something clobbers the things below it. We can certainly define semantics by rules of that kind, yet the result will never be satisfactory, because such mechanisms don't correspond to anybody's intuition. I guess what I am saying once again is: You can get bitten by the bug of solving puzzles for puzzles' sake.

Daylight: Can you explain the relationship between Floyd's work and your later work on LR(k) languages?

Knuth: By 1965, I had already written up most of what I wanted to say about context-free languages in *The Art of Computer Programming* [39]. When I was finishing the draft of Chapter 10, which is about parsing, I was rereading Bob Floyd's papers and studying two or three Ph.D. dissertations on the subject. One thesis, by my friend Bill Lynch at the University of Wisconsin (who had collaborated with me on RUNCIBLE), was about certain kinds of grammars for which parsing was possible without backing up.

My draft chapter included Floyd's theories about precedence grammars and about what later was called Floyd productions or Floyd–Evans productions; and it also included some original material that I published later in the paper "Top-down syntax analysis" [42]. As I finished presenting this material, the higher-level notion that became known as LR(k) languages came to me; and I said to myself "Wait, this is way out there. It generalizes all these Ph.D. theses that I read. It's really interesting, but it is far too difficult to include in Chapter 10. It's beyond the scope of my book."

I wrote a long letter to Bob Floyd, summarizing the ideas and explaining that they seem to provide a nice characterization of exactly when it is possible to recognize syntax structures in one scan from left to right without backing up, while looking ahead at k or fewer characters. It was a 12-page letter, written between

Christmas of 1964 and New Year's Day of 1965, just after I'd finished the draft of Chapter 10. (I was hoping to finish the book before my son was born, which was in July of 1965, so I was working day and night.)

Shortly afterwards I was invited to give a lecture at Stanford, I think in February 1965. I was sitting in a dorm room at Stanford, preparing my lecture for the next day, and I had just seen the abstract of a new paper by Ginsburg and Greibach, which was about something they were calling deterministic languages. It suddenly dawned on me that their notion of deterministic languages was probably equivalent to my notion of LR(k) languages, but defined in quite a different way. So I stayed up late that night, thinking about the connection. When I gave my lecture at Stanford the next day, I think I stated the theorem wrong; but I've found that giving a lecture always sharpens and improves my ideas.

Shorty afterward I wrote the paper [36] about LR(k). My exposition in that paper was unfortunately rather awkward, because I didn't yet have a good understanding of the theory, but it was the best I could do at the time. I had intentionally been saving the simpler theory about top-down parsing for the book, instead of preparing it for journal publication; but I wrote up the LR(k) theory right away, because it was too hard for my book.

Now, of course, when I get to Chapter 10 in the real book — assuming that I live long enough — LR(k) will sort of be the beginning of the story. In 1964, I'd been going through and surveying what was then known about parsing, and none of the other researchers knew of all the different aspects that I had uncovered while writing the chapter because I was putting together those facts for the first time. It turned out that the LR(k) theory was a synthesis that worked. But it didn't become well known and popular until Mike Harrison and Frank DeRemer had figured out what I was talking about and explained it better.

Daylight: That's an example of generalizing, seeking unification.

Knuth: Yes, finding the essence of different approaches, what makes them tick. All of a sudden you see that one special case has the same sort of little conceptual principle as another, and many cases come tumbling together.

Daylight: Did you also dig into the life of Post?

Knuth: Not at that time. I knew nothing about his tragic life.

Daylight: Do you recall the topic of tag systems?

Knuth: Only vaguely. I never played around with tag systems. I thought they were interesting, but Post's Correspondence problem was easiest to apply.

Daylight: Later, in 1968, you wrote about your Turingol language in 'Semantics of Context-Free Languages' [38].

Knuth: Yes, as an example of semantics. I decided that I would base an example language on Turing machines, because Turing machines have the simplest "machine language" for which semantics is already well defined.

Daylight: A couple of months ago in Manchester, you told me that you really started to appreciate Turing's work only after you had read about his programming work.

Knuth: His manual for the Mark I. Yes.

Daylight: But, based on what we've just been discussing, I see you also had a lot of appreciation for Turing's theoretical work.

Knuth: That's true. But I had previously looked at him as one-dimensional.

Daylight: You wrote in your 1967 article 'The Remaining Trouble Spots in ALGOL 60' that:

> The use of the word "undefined" [...] is highly ambiguous, and under some interpretations it leads to undecidable questions that would make ALGOL 60 truly impossible to implement. [...]
>
> By a suitable construction, the latter condition can be made equivalent to the problem of deciding whether or not a Turing Machine will ever stop. [47, p.171]

Knuth: Here I was assuming that computer-literate readers do know that the Halting Problem is beyond implementation.

Daylight: Likewise, in your 1977 account about the early development of programming languages, you wrote:

> Of all the papers we shall consider, Böhm was the only one who gave an argument that his language was universal, namely, capable of computing any computable function. [47, p.34]

Knuth: In this connection I want to say a lot more about programming language history.

First of all, at the Syracuse conference where I met Floyd in 1962, I presented a paper called 'A History of Writing Compilers' [35]. I think a reviewer in *Computing Reviews* said later that "It was a lousy conference. For example, one person presented a paper about the history of writing compilers, but what he really described was the history of his writing one compiler."

Well, that was not quite true, but it is true that my historical research was lousy. I knew hardly anything about the important developments that now are covered in my 1977 paper 'The Early Development of Programming Languages' [54]. I had known only the things that had come to my consciousness when I was an undergraduate. Many, many other pioneers had been contributing to the world of programming, and I'd been totally oblivious to them. So I felt guilty about having published such a superficial paper about the history of writing compilers.

During the next year, I started looking more and more at source materials. I wrote to Rutishauser, Glennie, and to another correspondent who had told me about Curry's work (see e.g. [12, 13]) — I don't think I ever wrote directly to Haskell Curry. And whenever a correspondent would refer to somebody else, I'd chase down that lead. Heinz Rutishauser told me about Konrad Zuse, so I wrote to Zuse. I got to know Andrei Ershov. All of these things were intended to make up for my amateurish attempt in 1962. Oh, it was Ed Blum — he was the guy who told me about Curry's unpublished work of 1949 and 1950.

The historical survey that I published in 1977 was certainly one of the most fascinating papers that I've ever worked on. To get history right, you have to try to get into the minds of all the creators of the ideas that are being discussed. Of all the papers I've written, I rank this one among the top three in terms of difficulty, but I greatly enjoyed working on it.

Now, you're mentioning Böhm here. He was the only one of the early authors I cited who explicitly mentioned the notion of universality.

Daylight: What about Carr and Gorn?

Knuth: I don't know what Carr did. But Saul Gorn was always strange. [Pause] I never was able to understand much of what he said. He was considered to be a senior researcher and I never knew why. He always was at the meetings but I never got any insight from anything that he said. Well, maybe once or twice. But in retrospect I think he was basically not a computer scientist.

Daylight: He influenced Perlis a lot.

Knuth: Perlis was definitely a computer scientist.

Daylight: Going back to your remark about Böhm that's quoted above, it's interesting to note that, at some point, you looked at the history of automatic programming with this theoretical question of universality in the back of your mind.

Knuth: Yes, by 1977 I had gotten older. When I was young, I was more like a machine. During the year that I had spent in Princeton before coming to Stanford, 1968/69, I'd started reading literature that I wasn't required to read: books by people like Dostoyevsky — I hated his work, but I read it anyway — and Tolstoy — whose work I loved. All of a sudden I was seeing more of the world and thinking about other stuff. I don't think that I had any of those qualities when I was young.

Daylight: In your 1977 paper, you also referred to E. K. Blum's work on ADES (1955–1956) and mentioned that it was based on Kleene's ideas and, in general, on the theory of recursive functions.

Also the name C. C. Elgot pops up in this context. Was this work influential at the time?

Knuth: Hardly anybody outside of Blum's local community ever heard about ADES. Ed Blum is professor at the University of Southern California. He is mainly known for being the editor of the *Journal of Computer & System Sciences*. He's a hard-working and successful editor, but not a researcher.

Daylight: Could you say something about the CUCH language, which Böhm presented in Vienna in 1964 [4]?

Knuth: The CUCH was based on a mixture of Curry's and Church's work; Böhm became enamored of such ideas when he went to Rome.

Daylight: I don't see much lambda calculus in your own research. Is that a fair assessment?

Knuth: Not quite, because I wrote this paper 'Examples of Formal Semantics' [40]. [Knuth browses through one of his books, which Daylight has brought with him.] Here it is, Chapter 18 in my book *Selected Papers on Computer Languages* [47]. I give two examples there, one of which is a formal definition of lambda calculus via attribute grammars. I am claiming here that this is the way people should define lambda expressions, since my proposed definition nicely matches human intuition. (Then the paper continues with 'Turingol revisited'.)

But it's true that I don't have much about the lambda calculus in my work. I learned about lambda calculus from Peter Wegner in the late 1960s.

By the way, since we have the book out, let me show you where I used the name of Peter Naur's daughter in my definition of Turingol, as part of a list of example identifiers. [Knuth browses through the book.] Here it is: *marilyn, jayne, birgitte* [47, p.393]. Birgitte refers to Peter's oldest daughter. You can use your imagination to figure out the identities of Marilyn and Jayne. Oops, there's a missing comma here. I'd better correct that error.

Daylight: In your 1967 paper 'The Remaining Trouble Spots in ALGOL 60', you wrote about the generality of procedures:

When ALGOL 60 was first published in 1960, many new features were introduced into programming languages, primarily with respect to the generality of "procedures". It was quite difficult at first for anyone to grasp the full significance of each of the linguistic features with respect to other aspects of the language; therefore people would commonly discover ALGOL 60 constructions they had never before realized were possible, each time they reread the Report. Such constructions often provided counterexamples to many of the usual techniques of compiler implementation, and in many cases it was possible to construct programs that could be interpreted in more than one way. [47, p.155]

Knuth: That passage is primarily about the call-by-name construction.

Daylight: I'm particularly interested in your comments about real arithmetic in ALGOL 60. You wrote:

The precision of arithmetic on **real** quantities has intentionally been left ambiguous [. . .]. In an interesting discussion, van Wijngaarden [65] has presented arguments to show, among other things, that because of this ambiguity it is not necessarily true that the relation '3.14 = 3.14' is the same as **'true'** in all implementations of ALGOL. We have already mentioned that ambiguities as such are not necessarily undesirable [. . .]

Thus a good language need not be unambiguous. But of course when intentionally ambiguous elements are introduced, it is far better to state specifically what the ambiguities are, not merely to leave them undefined, lest too many people think they are writing unambiguous programs when they are not. [47, p.167–168]

Knuth: In the 1960s there was no IEEE standard for floating point computations. So it would have been impossible to say what you would get when you computed, say, the sum of two real numbers. The language designers couldn't guarantee consistency from one computer to another, because there was no standard until 20 years later. They left real arithmetic ambiguous so that people would still be able to write programs. Their feeling, I believe, was that a numerical analyst would therefore be cautious and try to make methods portable even though existing machines were incompatible.

Daylight: I believe that in the official definition of ALGOL 60 [2], integer arithmetic is considered to be pure arithmetic ...

Knuth: ... up to overflow I suppose.

Daylight: No, they only mention overflow for the arithmetic on real numbers [2, Section 3.3.6].

Knuth: I see. Evidently I've forgotten this aspect of the language. I wonder what my compiler of 1960 did?

Similar instances of undefined arithmetic occur in lots of of programming languages. For example, the C language doesn't define the quotient of −1 divided by 2. The semantics of this operation is expressly unspecified. You have to avoid such quotients if you want to be sure that the same result will be obtained on a variety of computers.

Daylight: We still have that problem today.

Knuth: Yes, and partly because, when C was defined, many computers used ones' complement arithmetic instead of two's complement arithmetic. So a negative number would be represented in different ways on different machines.

Daylight: Is it correct that most of the constructs in the C language are defined in terms of an arbitrary but finite machine?

Knuth: C does have quantities such as *maxint* as part of the Standard Library, to be instantiated by the preprocessor at compile time.

The C language provides a way for programmers to check whether or not a buffer overflow has occurred. If programmers don't use this feature, they have to hope that their programs are OK. But the programs will run differently on different machines. This causes problems in reliability.

We're faced with consequences of undefined semantics all the time. For example, many web pages work properly only with Microsoft Explorer if the person who designed them used Microsoft's software; that person had no easy way to know what Firefox would do with the same web page.

Daylight: Around 1963, you designed an artificial machine called MIX for use in *The Art of Computer Programming*. Your incentive to do so was that machines were changing rapidly. In order to write a book on compilers, you needed to fix the target machine. You wanted an ideal machine for portability reasons.

Knuth: Right. Later, when I wrote TEX, I was extremely careful about portability. I completely avoided floating point arithmetic in places where the computations could affect page layout. Instead, I implemented my own arithmetic for the internal computations, using integer operations only, and I checked boundary conditions so that my programs would be machine-independent. I wanted to be sure that everybody who uses TEX would get the same results, regardless of the country they lived in and regardless of the operating system they were using, either now or fifty years from now.

Daylight: To check boundary conditions, you need to have something like C's *maxint*.

Knuth: Yes, and for the floating point I had to write code like I had been doing long ago for the runtime library of the Burroughs 205. I had to implement arithmetic operations that don't depend on undefined notions of rounding. Likewise, the fonts produced by my programs are generated in such a way that every machine will produce precisely the same result.

Daylight: Could you help me interpret Table 3.1? It's from Harry Huskey's chapter in *Advances in Computers, Volume 5.* What do the "No limit" entries actually mean? Why are they only present in ALGOL and SMALGOL (and to a lesser extent in NELIAC and PHILCO ALTAC)? Do the entries resemble a machine-independent philosophy?

| | Symbols in identifiers | | Integer range | Real range | Array dimensions | Symbols per statement | Labels |
	Max. no.	Significant					
ALGOL	No limit	All	No limit	No limit	No limit	No limit	Integer identifier
SMALGOL	No limit	1st 5 + last 5	10^{11}	$10^{-38}, 10^{38}$	No limit	No limit	Identifier
NELIAC	No limit	1st 15	10^{11}	$10^{-38}, 10^{38}$	1	No limit	Identifier
MAD	6	6	10^{11}	$10^{-38}, 10^{38}$	2	No limit	Identifier
1620 FORTRAN	5	5	10^{4}	$10^{-50}, 10^{49}$	2	72	1–9999
1620 GOTRAN	4	4	10^{3}	$10^{-50}, 10^{49}$	1	72	1–999
650 FORTRAN	5	5	10^{10}	$10^{-50}, 10^{50}$	2	125	1–9999
650 FORTRANSIT	5	5	10^{10}	$10^{-50}, 10^{50}$	2	125	1–999
7070 FORTRAN	6	6	10^{10}	$10^{-50}, 10^{50}$	3	660	0–99999
705 FORTRAN	6	6	10^{10}	$10^{-50}, 10^{50}$	3	660	1–99999
704/7090 FORTRAN	6	6	32767	$10^{-38}, 10^{38}$	3	660	1–32767
HONEYWELL	6	6	2^{44}	$10^{-77}, 10^{76}$	3	660	1–32767
PHILCO ALTAC	7	7	32767	$10^{-600}, 10^{600}$	4	No limit	Identifier
CDC FORTRAN	8	8	10^{14}	$10^{-308}, 10^{308}$	3	700^{a}	1–9999

[a]Ten cards

Table 3.1: Comparison of Algorithmic Languages Including a Variety of Fortrans [33, p.370].

Knuth: "No limit" means that the compiler was supposed to allow arbitrary inputs, except when the size would exceed the actual capacity of the computer. For example, an array in ALGOL or SMALGOL could in principle have a million dimensions, if you had a machine big enough to hold such an enormous array. (Nobody did, of course.) The language gave no limits, but the operating system would kick you off if the resources you asked for weren't available. By contrast, arrays in ForTransit could never have more than two dimensions under any circumstances.

4. Structured Programming

Daylight: Around 1969, structured programming changed your life and Bob Floyd's life. You wrote:

> There was a revolutionary new way to write programs that came along in the 1970s, called structured programming. It was a different way than we were used to when I had done all my compilers in the 1960s. Bob and I, in a lot of our earliest conversations at Stanford, were saying, "Let's go on the bandwagon for this. Let's understand structured programming and do it right." [21, p.28]

Did structured programming in this context refer to Dijkstra's structured programming, or was it more broadly construed?

Knuth: In my 1974 article 'Structured Programming with go to Statements' [43] I explain what I mean by structured programming: to understand a program in terms of its structure. By doing so, we can deal with complexity, because a complex thing can be built of simple parts that are connected in simple ways. That's what I call the structure. The fact that goto statements might be present does not contradict the fact that a program can have structure. That's the intuitive idea I had.

Other people just defined structured programming as goto-less programming. Their view was like the movement for zero population growth, where people would say "just don't have any more kids" without saying anything about the quality of life. I regard structured programming as a discipline that is not quantitative but rather qualitative; I focus on structural connections between different parts.

Daylight: That's your 1974 article, but your interest started in 1969.

Knuth: Well, more likely in 1970. I think it started for me when I read Dijkstra's original Notes on Structured Programming [19], and heard him lecture on the subject at the Newcastle seminar in September of that year [20]. Of course, the topic had been in the air ever since he had published his famous letter about "harmful" go to statements in 1968 [18]. As a result, one of the first papers Bob Floyd and I wrote when we got together at Stanford was about avoiding goto statements in a decent way [52].

My interest intensified greatly at the end of 1972, when Dijkstra's notes were combined with extensive additional material by Tony Hoare and Ole-Johan Dahl and published in the book *Structured Programming* [14]. That book was a great monument. I composed long "open letters" to its authors, commenting on various points they had brought up [51].

Daylight: The book by Dahl, Dijkstra, and Hoare seems to have been as influential as your first encounters with Perlis's IT compiler and with SOAP.

Knuth: Yes, it was revolutionary in my thinking. For sure.

Daylight: Why was this?

Knuth: Dijkstra showed how you can clearly and cleanly decompose a complex thing into simpler parts. I didn't buy all his claims about top-down programming; I agree with Peter [Naur] that you actually have your mind on the goal too (cf. [16]). If you had started out with a slightly different goal, you would have decomposed the problem in a different way. But still, the result of the decomposition is wonderful. And I now use those concepts daily in what I call Literate Programming [45], which is structured programming plus as much human intuition as I can add. My current programs generally describe what worked and what didn't work, and they proceed both bottom-up and top-down.

Daylight: In your 1984 paper 'Literate Programming' [44], you took the prime-number example of Dijkstra and presented it in the very same way that he had, that is, with these separate levels. [K: Right.] But in your 1974 article 'Structured Programming with go to Statements' there is no decomposition into levels; instead, you talk about program manipulation systems.

Knuth: That's true. Some people like program manipulation systems, but that concept hasn't really flourished. I had the feeling that people would enjoy high-level manipulations, but I probably guessed wrong. I never followed through on those ideas, because I became distracted by other things.

Daylight: In your 1974 article, you wrote:

> [Around 1969] I was still not convinced that all goto statements **could** or **should** be done away with, although I ..." [43, p.264, Daylight's emphasis]

Did you intentionally distinguish between "could" and "should"?

Knuth: Yes; but now that I look at it, I was wrong. I certainly was convinced that they *could* be done away with. My use of rhetoric wasn't legitimate there.

Daylight: Realizing that they can be done away with does require some insight. Do you think most of your colleagues shared that insight?

Knuth: A lot of other people were blindly convinced that fewer goto's was the measure of quality.

Daylight: Okay, so you didn't mean anything theoretical with "could be done away with". It's just that when I look at Fred Brooks's words, from 1975, he did refer to a theoretical connotation of goto-less programs. He wrote:

> Another important set of new ideas for designing the bugs out of programs derives largely from Dijkstra [Structured Programming], and is built on a theoretical structure by Böhm and Jacopini. Basically the approach is to design programs whose control structures consist only of loops defined by a statement such as DO WHILE, and conditional

> portions delineated into groups of statements marked with brackets and conditioned by an IF...THEN...ELSE. *Böhm and Jacopini show these structures to be theoretically sufficient;* Dijkstra argues that the alternative, unrestrained branching via GO TO, produces structures that lend themselves to logical errors. [5, p.144, Daylight's emphasis]

Knuth: That was the common idea by the people who didn't really . . . Brooks was a manager. There was another guy in IBM who was very sharp and was promoting structured programming.

Daylight: Mills.

Knuth: Harlan Mills, yes. Brooks knew that structured programming was helping his groups, but he was basing his words on what he had heard.

You and I were talking about the Böhm-Jacopini theorem in Manchester a couple of months ago. I was wrong when I downplayed it completely. Even though a lot of us knew that it was not at all a significant result, more than 90% of all working programmers believed that it was an important theorem, and Brooks's words illustrate this.

The popular view was misguided because the Böhm-Jacopini theorem lets you get rid of the goto statements, but it produces a goto-less program that has absolutely no structure whatsoever.

Daylight: Historically, the theorem has influenced many people, but incorrectly.

Knuth: Yes, for the wrong reasons. I wrote a paper that was presented in 1971 called 'The Dangers of Computer Science Theory' [41]. I gave many examples of theorems that were valid, but completely misunderstood by the community.

Daylight: So one misconception was to think that the programming-language structures in the Böhm-Jacopini paper were practically sufficient.

Knuth: The state model of a Turing machine makes it change to a newly specified state after every step of a computation. So the operation of a Turing machine basically consists of one goto after another, separated only by rudimentary tests and assignments. Böhm and Jacopini simply observed that one could emulate a Turing machine in a high-level language without using the words 'go to'. Indeed, you can just say: *while true do the following: if state=1 and if you're scanning symbol A then set state equal to 5; else* ... and so on. There are no explicit goto statements here, but spaghetti-like connections are everywhere. So their construction had nothing to do with structured programming. It was the opposite of structured programming.

When you're talking about structures in terms of the control structures of a programming language, you're not necessarily talking about structures that help you to understand your program. You're only talking about structures that the language's "hardware" permits you to use. Böhm and Jacopini's notion of "structure" had nothing in common with the true meaning of program structure.

Daylight: Program transformations play an important role in your article 'Structured Programming with go to Statements'.

Knuth: It's very helpful to be able to think of doing things at the high level, instead of at the low level — that is, to think in the language with which you're working, instead of in some intermediate language. Compiler writers work with some internal representation of the code when they are optimizing; they're moving things out of loops and so on. But you can also imagine doing such transformations in the source code, and asking a programmer for hints about how to proceed. I gave an example before: $x \neq y$ versus $x > y$. Sometimes those two things are equivalent in the algorithm and, if so, a compiler is allowed to substitute a more efficient program for the original one. Many transformations are almost always correct, but they have exceptions. If compiler writers could ask a programmer "By the way, may I assume this ... ?" then they could use a machine much better. I was hoping that such source-level communications would help solve many problems, but in retrospect my proposal was probably not based on the right psychology for the world's programmers.

Daylight: I know people who are still interested in program manipulation systems.

Knuth: Right. We can learn a lot by thinking about them, but I don't think they've yet been incorporated into successful products at the user level.

Daylight: You distinguished between the high level of the source code and the low level of the machine. In Dijkstra's structured programming, most of his programming work is in levels higher than the source code; it is in what he calls "descriptions" or "levels of abstraction".

Knuth: Those levels are good, they correspond to real structure. That's not a Böhm–Jacopini type of structure.

Daylight: You had such levels of abstractions in your 'Literate Programming' article, but you didn't have any of that in your 1974 article 'Structured Programming with go to Statements'.

Knuth: In the 1974 paper I was considering fragments of programs rather than total programs. That paper doesn't explain how to calculate prime numbers. It presents a sub-problem that seems to need goto's, but it doesn't consider the whole context. I only focused on the goto aspect, instead of looking at a complete problem. I did consider some interesting examples of coroutines, but again that was a matter of trying to achieve a given structure, and to understand that structure even though a goto is present.

Part of the book that I am writing now involves what we call backtracking. Sometimes you're changing a data structure in preparation for a later step, but all of a sudden you notice that some contradiction has been discovered in the middle of a loop. You also have the inverse loop, which undoes the effect of the first loop. If you need to undo an unfinished loop, you're in an awkward situation because you have to jump into the middle of the second loop. (You don't want to undo all of the operations — you're only faced with undoing those that were done before the contradiction arose.) Jumping into the middle of a loop is a worse sin than an ordinary goto; yet it is the correct way to proceed in such a situation. My 1974 paper tried to explain why such jumps are indeed legitimate in the context of backtracking.

Floyd had a beautiful paper about this subject, called 'Nondeterministic Algorithms' [27]. If we need to jump into another loop *and* we can understand why, then there is no reason to forbid the jump. There are times when going into the middle of a loop is not only the best thing to do, but it is also easy to understand if you know what the problem is.

The point I am trying to make is that instead of talking about program refinement, I was trying to show instead that goto statements are sometimes consistent with well-understood structure.

When Tony Hoare first formalized Pascal, he didn't provide any rules for goto statements, which had become statements of ill repute. But, then, after he had read the draft of my paper, he said "You know Don, actually I've now found a very simple way to define the semantics of the goto statement, and I wish I hadn't thought of it." He realized that you could have structure with goto statements. He could have added this rule and have thereby obtained a more complete formalization of Pascal.

Daylight: Concerning Hoare's formalization of the goto statement, there are at least two possible interpretations here. One is that his formalism isn't good enough because goto statements can easily be formalized after all. The other one is the one you mentioned, namely that not all goto's are bad because they are not difficult to formalize.

Towards the end of your 1974 article, you explained how Dijkstra had reacted positively to your use of the goto statement. You wrote:

> It is hard for me to express the joy that this letter [by Dijkstra] gave me; it was like having all my sins forgiven, since *I need no longer feel guilty about my optimized programs.* [43, p.286, Daylight's emphasis]

Knuth: You have to take that with a little grain of salt. I wasn't feeling as bad, when writing an optimized program with a goto statement, as Dijkstra was feeling when he read the IBM specifications. [K&D: Laughter] But, yes, it was nice for me to know that I had gotten a little bit of absolution for my transgressions.

By the way, speaking of Dijkstra and confessions, I once gave a lecture in Eindhoven, in one of his seminars. I wrote on the blackboard and was describing an algorithm for pattern matching. I wrote down steps 1, 2, and 3, in English. Then when I got to step 4, I stopped dramatically, and asked, "Is it allowed to use goto statements in this room?" And Edsger said, "I saw it coming." [K&D: Laughter] I had intentionally planned this.

Daylight: I heard that you had worked on de Bruijn's Automath. Is that right?

Knuth: I never published anything about Automath, but I did write de Bruijn at least one long letter about the subject. I wanted him to put types into Automath, sort of like class structures; I guess you could call it object-oriented Automath. I gave him an example of a proof about equivalence relations in which such types were particularly helpful. As far as I could tell, there was no way to have such a nice proof in Automath as it was.

I thought my suggestion was a reasonable extension to what he had. But he didn't like it because he wasn't writing the programs. He feared that his programmers would find it troublesome — I don't remember exactly why.

In Automath you can do something like say that x is an integer. You can also say that x is a prime number. But you have to re-prove everything that you proved for integers if you want to use the prime numbers as a subclass of the integers. The proofs for the integers don't carry over to the prime numbers. I tried unsuccessfully to convince him to add such an object-oriented extension to Automath.

Daylight: When was this?

Knuth: During the late 1960s.

5. Software Pioneers

Daylight: Can you tell me something about Arthur Burks?

Knuth: I had some correspondence with him about the history of programming languages. Early on he had invented an interesting language oriented towards business data processing. He and Herman Goldstine were later at each other's throats with respect to the Iowa machine [of Atanasoff]. I wasn't involved with that myself.

Daylight: I've got a whole list of people here. I'd like to know which people from this list you knew well during the 1950s or 1960s.

Knuth: Ingerman I knew a little bit. I didn't know Post. Did I meet Church? I think I did meet him. He was a white-haired man who spoke very slowly.

Dana Scott I know very well at present, and I now see him often. But he left Stanford just before I arrived, so I didn't interact with him in the 1960s.

I talked a few times to Chris Strachey in 1967, just before meeting Peter Naur. Strachey was at the big conference on simulation languages in Norway. Many years later I read a lot of Strachey's archives at Oxford, where they are collected in the Bodleian Library. I looked especially at some of the programs he wrote for the Manchester machine.

Heinz Rutishauser I talked to a little bit. He programmed Zuse's machine in Zürich. Konrad Zuse I met in 1976, after having carefully read his large book about the Plankalkül. The amazing programs in the Plankalkül for parsing, for playing chess, and for floating point arithmetic show that he was really well ahead of others. He was, like Turing, one of the first real computer scientists.

Bernie Galler made a great contribution by founding the IEEE *Annals of the History of Computing*. He wasn't a top researcher. He worked with other people to make the MAD compiler — I think Bob Graham was really the brains behind that. Galler and Perlis wrote a paper about extensions to ALGOL for matrices and other complex data types [28]. It wasn't a brilliant work but it was very good for its time. Bernie's main contributions were organizational rather than research-oriented.

I knew Ned Irons. Besides the syntax-directed compiler, he also wrote the operating system of the computer that I used when I did classified work. That system was very idiosyncratic. Ned was a genius, but his intuition didn't match that of many other people. His programming language, called IMP, was the most terse that I've ever used. Instead of saying 'if $x > 0$ then $y := z$' you would say 'x+=>y<-z'; the 'x+' meant 'if $x > 0$' and the '=>' meant 'then'. The terseness of the language meant that it was almost impossible to read any program that you had written a month earlier. Your programs just looked like a bunch of squiggles on a page, without any perceivable structure.

IMP was also defined in its own language, and anybody could extend the language at any time. So a program that worked on Monday might not work on Tuesday because somebody else may have changed the language in the meanwhile. If you had a bug in your program, instead of giving an ordinary error message as we're used to, it would just say *ERROR ERROR ERROR* and stop. That's what would happen if you had made a syntax error. If your program compiled and you ran it but didn't give the right answer, then you'd have to check the machine language, because somebody may have extended the compiler to produce bad code.

So Irons's IMP language had all possible strikes against it. Yet it was the language of choice when we used that machine (the Control Data 6600), because Ned had also written the operating system and the debugger. The machine code that IMP generated was perfectly matched to his operating system and his debugging system. The alternative would have been to have a really good programming language but then it would have been incompatible with the system. We put up with all the idiosyncrasies because we could get our programs working faster. That was my experience with Ned Irons. I don't know anybody else like that in computer science.

Peter Wegner and I talked a lot about writing about textbooks. His idea was that I shouldn't write *The Art of Computer Programming* in the way that I had been doing it. Instead, he said, I should first write a short summary of everything and then expand each part. But I can't write confidently about something until I've surrounded that topic; then I try to boil it down afterwards. Peter and I sort of occupy opposite poles in that respect.

I only met Saul Rosen once or twice. I like his book on software [61].

Daylight: What about Landin?

Knuth: I didn't know Peter Landin at all. I saw him once at a conference. He was kind of a wild Englishman. He had a different view of the world than I did. Dana Scott is a versatile logician. I think Peter Landin was more one-sided.

Daylight: Didn't Landin and Scott both have a world view that differed from yours?

Knuth: It could be. The only paper I know by Landin is 'The Next 700 Programming Languages' [55]. Dana Scott was deriving elegant theorems about continuity and so on. But that was all a different world for me. It was closer to the right way than de Bakker's approach. Nevertheless, I still think that attribute grammars are the way to go.

On the other hand, people do have different brains. My preferences might very well not be the best approach for everybody.

To me, if formalism is just playing games and has rules that you can puzzle over, it is amusing but not substantial. The right formalism is something that matches the thinking process. I'm sure that there are different kinds of thinking processes. The formalism that matches my thinking process is different from the formalism that matched Peter Landin's thinking process.

I knew John McCarthy very well, of course. He and I would talk about something different every time we met. He was encyclopedic like Dijkstra. McCarthy loved to debate and I don't. We once had a debate about how to define semantics.[1].

Daylight: Can you say something about Tony Hoare's 1969 article 'An Axiomatic Basis for Computer Programming' [30]? I guess that was a different way of thinking for you?

Knuth: No. It was really much like Floyd's approach (cf. [26]), but Hoare worked in a way that blends better with the formalism. In Hoare's approach, you do the operations backwards instead of forwards. That was brilliant, I wouldn't have thought of it. Both Floyd and Hoare were very much ahead of their time in saying that we can really handle important programs and know that they are right, instead of just patching them as I said earlier.

Tony Hoare's first article on that subject in the *Communications of the ACM* was called 'Proof of a Program: FIND' [31]. I'm not sure whether it was in the published version or in the preprint that I saw, but I found at least two serious errors in his proof even though he always drafted his papers over and over again. When you set out to construct a really airtight formal proof, all of a sudden you are raising the bar: Your standards go way up. Thus in spite of all his careful revisions, there still were cases where he had failed to prove that every subscript of the array was in bounds, or something like that. Even though his paper probably presented the best program proof ever constructed up till that time, it still wasn't complete. That shows the difficulty of the problem.

Daylight: What then is your take on formal methods? Peter Naur was very suspicious of them.

Knuth: Peter said that formal methods would never get into industry. He was definitely wrong there. It just takes another generation before people start to understand what is going on.

---

[1]Editor's note: That story is explained in Knuth's book *Selected papers on Computer Languages* [47, p.433]

Figure 5.1: Peter Naur (right) visiting Donald Knuth at his home.
Picture taken in January 1975 by Jill Knuth.

My own take is that I prove things informally as I'm writing a
program. That is, I set up invariants and try to be careful that I
preserve those invariants. But I don't submit my program to a
checker. The fact that I know that these formal methods exist is a
huge help in my own programming.

I've heard about a number of examples where proof checker
programs have in fact been important, including industrial cases.
The change has been slow coming, but nowadays it's certainly not
a radical idea at all to check critical routines formally. Tony Hoare
is now promoting that kind of software as a Grand Challenge
(cf. [32]).

Daylight: Which brings us to Dijkstra's Pleasantness Problem [16,
p.77], and that's where Peter Naur is most critical. As soon as
you have a formal specification, you can, at least in principle,
work all formally. But ensuring that the formal specification
matches the original design intent (which is informal) remains
very problematic and is hardly investigated by formal methods
people.

Knuth: The formal specification may be lousy. But we still need a precise way to do a formal specification. The mistake would be to believe that precise specs are all that you have to do, that they are sufficient as well as necessary. And I think Edsger Dijkstra meant that, somehow, as human beings, we also want to be able to appreciate that we've got the right formal specification. We want a pleasant formal specification because it's the right formal specification. If it isn't, then these formal verifiers will verify that the wrong specification has been implemented. I couldn't develop TEX without also being the user of TEX and seeing that maybe I shouldn't have defined it this way.

Daylight: I'm a bit lost now. You can have a formal specification that is a bit wrong but —

Knuth: I'm saying: A formal specification is somehow right by definition, but it can be wrong because it's not pleasant. It can be wrong because it was a stupid way to define what you wanted. It was defining some rules where you could have defined a better rule.

Daylight: At some point in your career after having invented and implemented TEX, you started to work on Literate Programming. One of the things you did was to rewrite all your TEX code in accordance with this new Literate Programming style. Did you, in this new context, work with formal specifications?

Knuth: TEX is probably the worst example, because it's not entirely structured: TEX contains macros, and macros are notorious for not having to obey nested structure. For example, you can define a macro that has more left parentheses than right parentheses; TEX allows this. For some people, that's much worse than any other sin. Yet I believe that macros are important in order to make the language adaptable to many applications. Consequently any person who uses the macros has to be careful. I don't prevent people from doing bad things.

Some programmers don't like to give that much freedom to the user. To exaggerate a little bit, I think that the situation is analogous to the story of the Garden of Eden. Adam and Eve, having the knowledge of good and evil, got the ability to make mistakes; all of a sudden they were allowed to use goto statements and macros. Instead of only having a limited menu with things to click on, they could write programs.

Let me clarify what I mean by wrong specification. It might be that you are specifying how a tape recorder should respond when you push the buttons. It might be that pushing this one button not only starts the recording process but also turns off a light. It might be that human beings do better if the light were turned on instead. There is nothing incorrect about the specification that the light should go off, but it's psychologically a bad match to the user. So there are alternative formal specifications that are better. Now, after we've got a formal specification, we can see whether we've met that specification with our implementation, and that's a different problem from wondering whether that specification was a good interface between the user and the tape recorder.

Daylight: Oh, I see. That's what I would call the design intent. It's informal, it's stated in plain English. You can, of course, choose to specify it in a formal language. I think Peter Naur's point would be that if you've got a certain design intent in mind, then it is by no means obvious that it can adequately be captured in a formal specification.

Knuth: Peter does it all in one. He doesn't separate the two. In his mind it's all one thing. Dijkstra explicitly distinguished between a pleasantness part on the one hand, which is more psychological, and a formal automatable part on the other hand.

Daylight: Naur didn't like it that Dijkstra dismissively called the first problem the Pleasantness Problem and that he directed all his attention to the formal part. He was angry that Dijkstra called the Pleasantness Problem a non-scientific problem.

Knuth: Yes, that pushed Peter's button. [K&D: Laughter] In a weak moment, I too would ... For example, don't ask my opinion about philosophers. I couldn't discuss Heidegger and all those people.

Daylight: I'll add Heidegger to this list of people that we're discussing.

Knuth: No, no, please. [D: Laughter] Martin Gardner wrote a very nice book called *The Whys of a Philosophical Scrivener* [29]. Pretty much everything I know about philosophy is from the examples that he gives in that book. Europeans seem to give much more attention to isms than people of my generation in America do.

I think that of all these people on your list, the ones who have won Turing awards have deserved it the most. [K&D: Laughter] I also put de Bruijn really high. As I told you before you started recording, he was my mentor through much of my life. And Bob Floyd was an inspiration all the way through, too. He got a disease similar to Alzheimer's, starting in the 1990s. But before then, I learned an awful lot from him.

6. Historiography

Knuth: I recently had a bit of a fight with Martin Campbell-Kelly.[1] We've agreed to disagree, but I was appalled by the current trend in history of science: Today's historians are much more against what they call internal history, as opposed to external history.

Martin wrote a paper called 'The History of the History of Software' [6], and I was in tears before I got to the end of it. I couldn't even finish it, because I was so angry. I was enraged because his paper lists, year by year, two or three publications about the history of computer science and puts them into categories: technical, supply-side industrial, applications-oriented, or institutional/social/political. During the first years, more than half of those publications were technical. But during the last ten years, the number of technical papers dropped to zero. This sea change occurred over a period of 30 years, and Martin evidently applauds this trend. He now tells his students to concentrate on contexts, and to write for a nontechnical audience, rather than also to give some depth.

I find this trend also taking place in the history of science generally. For example, I studied the main science history journal, *Isis*, from 50 years ago and compared to what *Isis* has published during the past two years. I counted how many of the articles told what some scientists did and what their discoveries were and who influenced them, versus articles of the form 'What strategies did the scientist use in order to survive? And what was his sex life about?' And so on. [D: Laughter] You know, dumbing things down to a common denominator, but with zero content about the scientific discoveries themselves or the methods that were introduced.

---

[1] Editor's note: Martin Campbell-Kelly is a renowned historian of computing.

My take on this is that Martin Campbell-Kelly had written a good book and that *Nature* got somebody to review it, and the reviewer wasn't a computer scientist. That reviewer sort of said: "Why would anybody care about any of this stuff?" I think Martin was wounded by the review, and he decided from then on to write books that are for the 90% of the people, but not for the 10% who can understand computer science.

Historians of *mathematics* still carry the torch; they still retain mathematical content in their papers.

To me an ideal history certainly does not ignore context, but it is a combination of breadth and depth. You give a broad picture, and then you also take parts of the subject and zoom in so as to teach the reader some interesting aspect of science. By contrast, if you stay only shallow, it's just just as bad as being only deep. So to me, the ideal way to write history is to focus on some of the details and get into the real science, but also to explain the circumstances, such as the person's life and the influences. If necessary, you can explain when the scientist had to put on a suit. [D: Laughter] Those stories are good, but to me the main value of historians is that they are really good at scouting out archives and discovering good source materials. Then they can whet the reader's appetite to go find and study that source material. That's different from assuming that the historian is going to be the only one who will cover the story. No. Historians should write for readers who will also want to read some of the sources themselves.

That's my bias. In June of 2009 I gave a talk at Greenwich University, entitled "History of Mathematics versus History of Computer Science." Martin Campbell-Kelly was present, and of course I had corresponded with him about my concerns. I told you [in connection with John McCarthy] that I don't like debates. But still, I did want to get this argument off my chest. I started by saying that I was probably making a mistake in giving a contentious talk. Yet I wanted to explain how deeply I felt about all this and about why history is important to me. I described in detail what I admire about historians of mathematics and why I now worry about historians of computer science and historians of science in general.

I'd been promised that this talk would be tape recorded and available on the Internet. But alas, the organizers discovered afterward that their recorder was broken that day. So my lecture was lost, and I won't have time to give it again. (About 200 people were present, and somebody did record their own personal video of the first few minutes in order to post it on YouTube. However, all my attempts to discover the identity of that person have failed, nor have I any clue about whether he or she had recorded the whole thing.) I don't intend to write a paper on this topic, so I'm telling you today about my concerns.

Daylight: Leo Corry, a historian of mathematics, gave an invited talk in October 2012 in Brussels about the work of Derrick Lehmer, Alan Turing, and other mathematicians who were involved with early computations.[2] After his talk, I read several of his papers (see e.g. [10, 11]). I have become attracted to his work exactly because it focuses on the *technical* achievements of early mathematical programmers, something I miss in many other historical accounts. I believe this observation matches the point you just wanted to make.

Concerning Campbell-Kelly's 2007 article 'The History of the History of Software', I certainly disagree with his statement that your research on the studies of programming languages was "of the low-hanging-fruit variety" [6, p.44]. In fact, I don't know many people who could have conducted a similar study. I have immense respect for Campbell-Kelly's views, but, at times, I have the impression that he is appropriating "software history". For example, he writes that:

> Software history began with narrow but essential technical studies in the 1960s and 1970s. **We** then looked at the supply-side industry in the 1980s and 1990s. **We** have only just begun to study applications. [...] Software history is heading in the **right** direction, [...] [6, p.50, Daylight's emphasis].

---

[2]Editor's note: See "Turing in Context II" (www.computing-conference.ugent.be/tic2).

I know some very good historians who would much rather stick to the "narrow" technical accomplishments of the 1940s–1960s.

Knuth: Hopefully there will also be some for the "narrow" technical accomplishments made after 1970.

In writing *The Art of Computer Programming* [39], I tried to get the history of the technical ideas correct. But I learned that Maurice Wilkes was unhappy with what I had written. He opined that I just didn't "get it," that I had misrepresented the history with which he had been involved. For him, my accounts just didn't ring true, and I was missing the whole point.

I took his criticism very seriously and I made it a point to meet with him when he visited Stanford. We spent a couple of hours together. He told me about sources to read, and I started to read them. Later I got back with him and he said "OK, now I'm happy." That meant a lot to me, basically to have a second chance instead of being written off as a hopelessly incompetent chronicler of early work.

In a way, I'm sort of thinking: Maybe I can do the same favor for you. I gave you my reaction to your book [17] in Manchester. I can see that you're serious and energetic, and that you share my goals for preserving important aspects of history and passing them on to future generations. My recommendation is to aim for a good balance between breadth and depth. The definition of a good, liberal education is to know something about everything and everything about something.

Daylight: Well, I took your comments seriously. To add depth to my work, I'm going to the Saul Gorn archives in Pennsylvania in two weeks from now.

Knuth: Of course I don't claim to have a monopoly on truth. But I've tried to present my personal take on these issues so that you can compare my views to others. You don't have to agree, but you can exhibit the contrasting opinions, and you don't have to insist on anybody winning.

Daylight: No, that should never be the intention.

Thank you very much for this interview.

Knuth: You're welcome. Thanks for the stimulating questions!

Bibliography

[1] D.J. Albers and G.L. Alexanderson, eds. *Mathematical People: Profiles and Interviews*. 2nd. Wellesley, Massachusetts: A K Peters, 2008.

[2] J.W. Backus et al. "Report on the algorithmic language ALGOL 60". In: *Communications of the ACM* 3.5 (1960). Editor: P. Naur, pp. 299–314.

[3] Y. Bar-Hillel, M. Perles, and E. Shamir. "On formal properties of simple phrase structure grammars". In: *Zeitschrift für Phonetik, Sprachwissenschaft und Kommunikationsforschung* 14 (1961), pp. 143–172.

[4] C. Böhm. "The CUCH as a formal descriptive language". In: *IFIP Working Conference*. Baden, Sept. 1964.

[5] F.P. Brooks Jr. *The Mythical Man-Month*. Addison-Wesley, 1975.

[6] M. Campbell-Kelly. "The History of the History of Software". In: *IEEE Annals of the History of Computing* 29.4 (2007), pp. 40–51.

[7] N. Chomsky. *Syntactic Structures*. The Hague/Paris: Mouton, 1957.

[8] J. Cocke and M. Minsky. "Universality of Tag Systems with $P = 2$". In: *Journal of the ACM* 11.1 (1964), pp. 15–20.

[9] *Convention on Digital Computer Techniques*. Institution of Electrical Engineers. 1956.

[10] L. Corry. "Number Crunching vs. Number Theory: Computers and FLT from Kummer to SWAC (1850-1960), and beyond". In: *Archive for History of Exact Science* 62.1 (2008), pp. 393–455.

[11] L. Corry. "Hunting Prime Numbers from Human to Electronic Computers". In: *The Rutherford Journal — The New Zealand Journal for the History and Philosophy of Science and Technology*, rutherfordjournal.org 3 (2010).

[12] H.B. Curry. *On the Composition of Programs for Automatic Computing*. Memorandum 9806. Silver Spring, Maryland: Naval Ordnance Laboratory, 1949.

[13] H.B. Curry. *A Program Composition Technique as Applied to Inverse Interpolation*. Memorandum 10337. Silver Spring, Maryland: Naval Ordnance Laboratory, 1950.

[14] O.-J. Dahl, E.W. Dijkstra, and C.A.R. Hoare. *Structured Programming*. London and New York: Academic Press, 1972.

[15] M. Davis. *Computability and Unsolvability*. McGraw-Hill, 1958.

[16] E.G. Daylight. *Pluralism in Software Engineering: Turing Award Winner Peter Naur Explains*. Edited by E.G. Daylight, K. De Grave, and P. Naur, ISBN 9789491386008. Lonely Scholar, Oct. 2011.

[17] E.G. Daylight. *The Dawn of Software Engineering: from Turing to Dijkstra*. Edited by K. De Grave, ISBN 9789491386022. Lonely Scholar, 2012.

[18] E.W. Dijkstra. "Go To Statement Considered Harmful". In: *Letters to the Editor, Communications of the ACM* 11 (1968), pp. 147–148.

[19] E.W. Dijkstra. *Notes on Structured Programming*. Tech. rep. T.H.-Report 70-WSK-03. Second edition. Technische Hogeschool Eindhoven, Apr. 1970.

[20] E.W. Dijkstra. "The Art of Programming". In: *The Teaching of Programming at University Level: Proceedings of the Joint IBM/University of Newcastle upon Tyne Seminar held in the University Computing Laboratory 8th–11th September 1970*. Ed. by B. Shaw. University of Newcastle Upon Tyne. 1971, pp. 3–20.

[21] E. Feigenbaum. *Oral History of Donald Knuth*. Tech. rep. CHM Reference number: X3926.2007. Mountain View, California: Computer History Museum, 2007.

[22] R.W. Floyd. "A descriptive language for symbol manipulation". In: *Journal of the ACM* 8.4 (1961), pp. 579–584.

[23] R.W. Floyd. "On ambiguity in phrase structure languages". In: *Communications of the ACM* 5 (1962), pp. 526, 534.

[24] R.W. Floyd. "On the nonexistence of a phrase structure grammar for ALGOL 60". In: *Communications of the ACM* 5 (1962), pp. 483–484.

[25] R.W. Floyd. "The syntax of programming languages—A survey". In: *IEEE Transactions on Electronic Computers* EC-13.4 (1964), pp. 346–353.

[26] R.W. Floyd. "Assigning Meanings to Programs". In: *Proceedings of Symposia in Applied Mathematics*. Vol. 19. American Mathematical Society. 1967.

[27] R.W. Floyd. "Nondeterministic Algorithms". In: *Journal of the ACM* 14.4 (1967), pp. 636–644.

[28] B.A. Galler and A.J. Perlis. "Compiling matrix operations". In: *Communications of the ACM* 5.12 (1962), pp. 590–594.

[29] M. Gardner. *The Whys of a Philosophical Scrivener*. William Morrow and Company, Inc, 1999.

[30] C.A.R. Hoare. "An Axiomatic Basis for Computer Programming". In: *Communications of the ACM* 12.10 (1969), pp. 576–580.

[31] C.A.R. Hoare. "Proof of a Program: FIND". In: *Communications of the ACM* 14.1 (1971), pp. 39–45.

[32] C.A.R. Hoare. "The verifying compiler: A grand challenge for computing research". In: *J. ACM* 50.1 (2003), pp. 63–69.

[33] H.D. Huskey. "An Introduction to Procedure-Oriented Languages". In: *Advances in COMPUTERS*. Ed. by F.L. Alt and M. Rubinoff. Vol. 5. Academic Press, 1964.

[34] D.E. Knuth. "RUNCIBLE — Algebraic Translation on a Limited Computer". In: *Communications of the ACM* 2.11 (1959). Reprinted with corrections and an addendum in [47]., pp. 18–21.

[35] D.E. Knuth. "A History of Writing Compilers". In: *Computers and Automation* 11.12 (1962). Reprinted with corrections and an addendum in [47]., pp. 8–18.

[36] D.E. Knuth. "On the Translation of Languages from Left to Right". In: *Information and Control* 8 (1965). Reprinted with corrections and an addendum in [47]., pp. 607–639.

[37] D.E. Knuth. "The remaining trouble spots in ALGOL 60". In: *Communications of the ACM* 10 (1967). Reprinted with corrections and an addendum in [47]., pp. 611–618.

[38] D.E. Knuth. "Semantics of Context-Free Languages". In: *Mathematical Systems Theory* 2 (1968). Reprinted with corrections and an addendum in [47]., pp. 127–145.

[39] D.E. Knuth. *The Art of Computer Programming, Vol. 1.* Reading, Massachusetts: Addison-Wesley, 1968.

[40] D.E. Knuth. "Examples of Formal Semantics". In: *Symposium on Semantics of Algorithmic Languages*. Ed. by E. Engeler. Vol. 188. Lecture Notes in Mathematics. Berlin: Springer, 1971, pp. 212–235.

[41] D.E. Knuth. "The Dangers of Computer-Science Theory". In: *Logic, Methodology and Philosophy of Science IV*. Studies in Logic and the Foundations of Mathematics 74. Reprinted with corrections and an addendum in [46]. Amsterdam: North-Holland, 1971, pp. 189–195.

[42] D.E. Knuth. "Top-Down Syntax Analysis". In: *Acta Informatica* 1 (1971). Reprinted with corrections and an addendum in [47]., pp. 79–110.

[43] D.E. Knuth. "Structured Programming with go to Statements". In: *Computing Surveys* 6.4 (Dec. 1974). Reprinted with corrections and an addendum in [45]., pp. 261–301.

[44] D.E. Knuth. "Literate Programming". In: *The Computer Journal* 27 (1984). Reprinted with corrections and an addendum in [45]., pp. 97–111.

[45] D.E. Knuth. *Literate Programming*. Stanford, California: CSLI Publications, 1992.

[46] D.E. Knuth. *Selected Papers on Analysis of Algorithms*. Stanford, California: CSLI Publications, 2000.

[47] D.E. Knuth. *Selected Papers on Computer Languages*. Stanford, California: CSLI Publications, 2003.

[48]   D.E. Knuth. *Selected Papers on Design of Algorithms*. Stanford, California: CSLI Publications, 2010.

[49]   D.E. Knuth. *Companion to the Papers of Donald Knuth*. Stanford, California: CSLI Publications, 2011.

[50]   D.E. Knuth. *Selected Papers on Fun and Games*. Stanford, California: CSLI Publications, 2011.

[51]   D.E. Knuth. *A review of 'Structured Programming'*. Tech. rep. STAN-CS-73-371. Computer Science Department, Stanford University, June 1973.

[52]   D.E. Knuth and R.W. Floyd. "Notes on Avoiding 'go to' Statements". In: *Information Processing Letters* 1 (1971). Reprinted with corrections and an addendum in [47]., pp. 23–31.

[53]   D.E. Knuth, Jr. J.H. Morris, and V.R. Pratt. "Fast Pattern Matching in Strings". In: *SIAM Journal on Computing* 6 (1977). Reprinted with corrections and an addendum in [48]., pp. 323–350.

[54]   D.E. Knuth and L. Trabb Pardo. "The Early Development of Programming Languages". In: *Encyclopedia of Computer Science and Technology*. Ed. by J. Belzer, A.G. Holzman, and A. Kent. Vol. 7. Reprinted with corrections and an addendum in [47]. New York: Marcel Dekker, 1977, pp. 419–493.

[55]   P.J. Landin. "The Next 700 Programming Languages". In: *Communications of the ACM* 9 (Mar. 1966), pp. 157–166.

[56]   P. Naur. "Proof of Algorithms by General Snapshots". In: *BIT Nordisk Tidskrift for Informationsbehandling* 6 (1966). Reprinted in [58, Sec. 5.2]., pp. 310–316.

[57]   P. Naur. *Concise Survey of Computer Methods*. Chapter 1 reprinted in [58, Sec. 1.2]. Studentlitteratur, Lund, 1974.

[58]   P. Naur. *Computing: A Human Activity*. New York: ACM Press/Addison-Wesley, 1992.

[59]   D. Nofre. "Unraveling Algol: US, Europe, and the Creation of a Programming Language". In: *IEEE Annals of the History of Computing* 32.2 (2010), pp. 58–68.

[60]   E. Post. "Recursive unsolvability of a problem of Thue". In: *Journal of Symbolic Logic* 12 (1947), pp. 1–11.

[61]   S. Rosen, ed. *Programming Systems and Languages*. New York: McGraw Hill, 1967.

[62]   A.A. Sardinas and G.W. Patterson. "A necessary and sufficient condition for the unique decomposition of coded messages". In: *Convention Record of the 1953 National Convention, Part 8: Information Theory*. Institute of Radio Engineers. 1953.

[63]   A.M. Turing. "On Computable Numbers, with an Application to the Entscheidungsproblem". In: *Proceedings of the London Mathematical Society, 2nd series* 42 (1936), pp. 230–265.

[64]   A. van Wijngaarden. "Generalized ALGOL". In: *Annual Review in Automatic Programming*. Ed. by R. Goodman. Vol. 3. Pergamon Press, 1963, pp. 17–26.

[65]   A. van Wijngaarden. "Switching and Programming". In: *Switching Theory in Space Technology*. Ed. by H. Aiken and W.F. Main. Stanford University Press, 1963, pp. 275–283.

[66]   R.L. Wilder. *Introduction to the Foundations of Mathematics*. New York: Wiley, 1952.

Index

Also by Edgar G. Daylight:

Conversations

- Pluralism in Software Engineering: Turing Award Winner Peter Naur Explains
  2011 · ISBN 9789491386008

- Panel discussions I & II, held at the Future of Software Engineering Symposium
  2011 · ISBN 9789491386015

Full-length books

- The Dawn of Software Engineering: from Turing to Dijkstra
  2012 · ISBN 9789491386022

Find our latest publications at www.lonelyscholar.com.

LONELY SCHOLAR™
SCIENTIFIC BOOKS

CPSIA information can be obtained at www.ICGtesting.com
Printed in the USA
LVOW05s0101231214

420031LV00012B/82/P